DEVELOPING A METACOGNITIVE CURRICULUM

DEVELOPING A METACOGNITIVE CURRICULUM

EDITED BY

NATHAN BURNS

Sage

1 Oliver's Yard
55 City Road
London EC1Y 1SP

2455 Teller Road
Thousand Oaks
California 91320

10th Floor, Emaar Capital Tower 2
MG Road, Sikanderpur, Sector 26
Gurugram, Haryana – 122002
India

8 Marina View Suite 43-053
Asia Square Tower 1
Singapore 018960

Library of Congress Control Number: 2025943240

British Library Cataloguing in Publication data

A catalogue record for this book is available from the British Library

Editor: James Clark
Editorial assistant: Harry Dixon
Production editor: Rabia Barkatulla
Marketing manager: Lucy Sofroniou
Cover design: Wendy Scott
Typeset by: TNQ Tech Pvt. Ltd.
Printed in the UK

ISBN 978-1-0362-0581-2
ISBN 978-1-0362-0580-5 (pbk)

Contents

About the editor

Nathan Burns is a renowned teacher educator, working with schools, education organisations and educators across the world to develop high-quality teaching practice. Working in a number of UK-based schools, Nathan worked as a pastoral leader, More Able coordinator, metacognition lead, and lately, as a Head of Maths. During his time in the classroom, Nathan wrote two well-received books on metacognition – *Inspiring Deep Learning* and *Teaching Hacks* – exploring how the theory can be effectively applied in the classroom. Since leaving the classroom, Nathan now leads high-quality professional development. He works with schools across the United Kingdom to deliver training on metacognition, alongside efforts with Teach First and Ambition Institute to train up the next generation of teachers. Nathan also leads Maths-specific training for organisations including the Maths Hub. You will often find Nathan presenting research at the latest teaching conference, as well as online, posting on socials as Mr Metacognition.

About the contributors

Dr. David Boyce, a nationally respected expert and multi-award-winning UK physics teacher, holds a PhD from Leicester and MPhys from Lancaster. Chartered in five disciplines – including as a mathematician, scientist, and teacher – he teaches at Queenswood School, authors textbooks, is a keynote speaker, a boarding housemaster and a professional mountaineer.

Liam Bretag is an experienced teacher of German, Spanish, and French. He is Head of Modern Foreign Languages at a secondary school in Cheshire. He is passionate about teaching and learning strategies that increase engagement, challenge and progress for all students. He proactively uses metacognitive strategies in the classroom to enhance students' learning experiences.

Sarah Dowey is an experienced English teacher, leader, and examiner, working as National Lead for English at Astrea Academy Trust. Research for her PhD in Education centred on applying metacognition and cognitive science principles to learning, and she is passionate about developing ways to effectively use these approaches to foster expert learners and increase academic attainment.

Adam Goodwin is a Head of PE from Middlesbrough, having qualified in 2012 after studying at Durham University. Deeply passionate about teaching and learning, Adam has a strong interest in innovative pedagogical approaches that enhance engagement and drive achievement. A proud father to twins, Teddy and Tommy, Adam is committed to educational excellence and thrives on sharing ideas that inspire both staff and students.

Benjie Groom is a history teacher and Oak National Academy's subject lead for history. Before joining Oak to oversee the release of a fully resourced, free primary and secondary history curriculum, Benjie led several history departments across a variety of Lincolnshire schools. He was the history subject lead for a large secondary SCITT and has extensive experience in history curriculum design, pedagogy, and history-specific ITT.

Kirsten Johnson trained as a secondary music teacher at the Royal Scottish Academy of Music and Drama and went on to hold a variety of roles – Head of Music, Head of Performing Arts, Head of House, and a dedicated form tutor. She has since been awarded a CCT Fellowship, gained her CTeach Qualification and holds an NPQSL. She returned to Scotland as a classroom teacher in 2022 due to a downturn in health and has now found her feet (so to speak) as a wheelchair user. She is currently applying her years of evidence-based school improvement work to a new analytical career within the Emergency Services.

Jonathan Usherwood is the Head of Computing at Teach First. With nearly 14 years of experience as an ICT and computing teacher in West Yorkshire secondary schools, he transitioned to Teach First in 2022 as a subject development lead in computing, advancing to his current role in 2024. He holds a Master's in Education and is dedicated to inspiring and equipping the next generation of teachers, passionately working to bridge the educational disadvantage gap.

Lucy Williams is an experienced art teacher and senior mental health lead with a passion for encouraging and supporting students pursuing art careers. Lucy is an ardent advocate for the arts, its importance in the curriculum and as a vehicle for how learning arts practices support mental and emotional well-being.

Ryan Woolaston is an experienced mathematics teacher and school leader with 15 years' experience in UK and international education, currently teaching in Bangkok. Passionate about evidence-informed pedagogy and developing metacognitive strategies, Ryan regularly speaks at conferences, leads professional networks, and is currently writing *The Right Angle: Evidence-informed approaches for great maths teaching*.

Acknowledgements

My first acknowledgement, as ever, goes to my wife, Catherine. As I have now left the classroom to focus on metacognition full time, she is ever more at the mercy of my rants about the theory, and ideas for new training events. She attends conferences alongside me and is ever supportive when I have yet more book edits to do late into the evening. She is the perfect, Mrs Metacognition.

I must also acknowledge the wonderful contributors and their contributions to this book. Without them, and their expertise, this book would be nothing (well, six chapters and then a lot of blank space...). But through sharing their time and expertise, they have helped to bring to life the invisible and complex idea of metacognition, within a full suite of subject areas. I am sure that their insights will bring much needed concrete examples of metacognition in the classroom, supporting thousands of teachers worldwide.

Finally, I must thank Mary Myatt, Ruth Ashbee, and Claire Hill, who all took the time to sense check my chapters on curriculum. For all the reading and research in the world, there is nothing superior to getting insight from the experts, and these three really are the experts on curriculum. Thank you!

Introduction

They say that in life, death, and tax are the only two certainties. I think we can actually add a third factor to this – schools having curriculum development as an area for improvement in any given year. And why wouldn't they? The curriculum details what it is we are going to teach our students. It answers questions such as:

- What topics do we teach our students in different years?
- How will we sequence topics in order to ensure coherency?
- How can we develop the curriculum in order to support the improvement of subject specific skills, such as problem solving?
- How can we develop student mental models through an effective curriculum?
- How do we ensure that students cover all of the content as required by the National Curriculum?

If each year, we can make at least minor improvements to the curriculum that we are delivering to students, the subsequent outcomes for these students hence should improve. Additionally, the curriculum is our vehicle to embed many research-backed pedagogical methods, whether that be retrieval practice, being built in to key parts of the curriculum or opportunities for reading and oracy development being highlighted.

It is the curriculum, therefore, that offers the best opportunity for us to embed metacognition within our schools. It will be chapter 1, rather than this introduction, which waxes lyrical about the benefits of metacognition, but if you are reading this book right now, then you are probably already quite invested in this way of teaching.

You will have found, that within the literature on metacognition, that there is very little work on what metacognition looks like in the classroom. I've tried to address this. My first book, *Inspiring Deep Learning with Metacognition* focused on illuminating a number of high-quality strategies that could be implemented within the classroom in order to support metacognitive development of our students. My second book, *Teaching Hacks*, placed emphasis on the perennial problems of teaching, such as students lacking motivation, poor oracy skills, ineffective revision techniques and extended writing, and how metacognition provides us with an approach to help tackle this year-on-year issues. This third book is looking to extend this work. We understand that curriculum is important and provides us with the best vehicle in which to implement metacognition across our schools. But what does this look like? This book will provide you with the answer to this and many other questions.

This book will begin with an exploration as to the importance of metacognitive development within our schools, as well as a consideration as to what metacognition actually is, from a theoretical perspective. Following on from this, curriculum development more generally will be considered. What are the risks that we face with curriculum change and implementation? How do we identify exactly what we *ought* to be focusing on, and when we make changes, how do we ensure that these become embedded. Finally, how do we get the balance right between whole-school expectations, but also remaining true to the subtlety of subject disciplines? Following on from this, curriculum experts then explore strategies to develop metacognitive abilities in their subject area. The strategies chosen, across the areas of planning, monitoring, and evaluation originate from my first book. In each of these chapters, subject experts have identified the strategies that are most suitable for the content area, and provided numerous examples of where they can be built into the curriculum.

Across these chapter areas, you will hopefully develop an improved understanding of metacognitive theory, how metacognition and the curriculum align and exactly what metacognition looks like in your curriculum area. As ever with my work, the emphasis is on readability backed by research. This book should be one that you are able to dip in and out of and draw out key ideas that you know are underpinned by research. All in all, this book should be the one-stop-shop for all of your questions around metacognition and the curriculum.

Part I
Key concepts

1

Metacognitive theory

Nathan Burns

The why

The fact that you have picked up this book probably means you already know that metacognition is incredibly powerful. However, it is still crucial that we consider all of the benefits of metacognition. Firstly, there may be some benefits that you are not currently aware of. Secondly, and perhaps more importantly, when implementing a metacognitive curriculum, it is imperative that your staff understand 'the why'. The better that the staff understand the rationale for a change, the more likely that they are to be on board with said change. So, let's begin.

The first reason why metacognition needs to be a focus is due to the evidence presented by the Education Endowment Foundation (EEF). The EEF is an organisation which reviews research literature around a vast number of teaching theories and pedagogies. Their report on metacognition (Education Endowment Foundation, 2019), which summarised over 1500 papers, determined that metacognition was the most powerful teaching practice that we could introduce into our schools. This means that metacognition is more important, arguably, than anything else that we can do in school. The EEF report determined that effective metacognitive teaching could lead to an eight-month uplift in student attainment. If we think about this, eight months is almost equivalent to a whole school year. Though it would be hard to argue that metacognitive teaching will lead to a year's improvement for every student, one thing is clear: metacognitive teaching will lead to improved outcomes for our students.

There is a second key education organisation which also supports the development of metacognition in schools: Ofsted. Love them or loathe them, Ofsted have recently made changes to ensure that what they demand of schools is embedded within high quality research and evidence. One of the changes that they have made is to their expectations of teacher professional development, which now details that metacognition would be a key component of high-quality professional development (Ofsted, 2019). We, of course, do not want to make changes just to tick a box, but where these changes ensure that we are in line with evidence, we ought to be making them. When we have got two significant organisations, Ofsted and the EEF, who agree on the power of metacognition and of metacognitive development in our students, we need to sit up and listen. Metacognition is powerful and ought to be a focus.

Beyond these organisations is the actual literature. I've been fortunate, for the purposes of these books and university research, to have been able to engage with much of this. What is clear in this literature is how metacognition really does benefit all students. Research shows us, that regardless of an individual's socioeconomic background or their demographics, metacognitive improvements lead to improved school attainment. Furthermore, an individual's prior attainment does not limit the benefits of metacognitive teaching. Whether an individual is previously high attaining, lower attaining, or somewhere in the middle, improved metacognitive skills lead to improved outcomes. Moreover, SEN students can also benefit from metacognitive teaching. So long as the metacognitive teaching is developed in an effective and adaptive manner, these students will also benefit. It also doesn't matter about an individual's sex or their behaviour profile. Intriguingly, students with poorer levels of behaviour can also benefit from metacognitive development. Improved metacognitive skills, improves access to work, and thus allows an individual to be more academically successful. We know that behaviour can often be caused by an inability to access work. Therefore, improved metacognitive skills, allowing students to access the work better can in turn lead to improved behaviour. Overall, the literature shows that all of our students can benefit from improved infinitive cognitive teaching. This is exactly the sort of pedagogy that we should spend time working on. Something that will improve the outcomes for all of our students.

Another key consideration of metacognition is the cost. or rather the fact that it doesn't cost anything. All too often in education we find an approach that can help, but that has a price tag which is prohibitive for schools. Fortunately, this is not true of metacognition. There is no programme to buy, textbooks to source, or subscription to pay. Apart from the cost of time, there are no financial costs which stop a school from prioritising this area as one for staff and students to developing.

You may think that we are done there. But we are not! Another advantage of metacognition is that it works across all phases. Metacognitive development is not limited to teenagers, and in fact can be found developing in students as young as two or three years old. It will become clearer later on in the chapter, but as soon as an individual starts showing cognitive action, metacognitive development can follow. This therefore means that regardless of the age of student that you work with, metacognitive development can be one of your top priorities. Also means that any work done in one key stage can be developed at the next key stage regardless of whether the student is staying at the same school, or moving to a new one.

Importantly for this book, metacognition is also shown to work across the curriculum. Sometimes it may seem easier to develop in maths and science, but later on this book will show you how it can be developed in every curriculum area. The main benefit here, is that metacognition can be a whole school focus. There is nothing worse than implementing a new idea across a whole school, that just doesn't suit every curriculum area. We are fortunate, that in this scenario, metacognition can, and should, be developed across every curriculum area.

More specifically, metacognition is also shown to improve an individual's ability to problem solve. Once again, just why this occurs will become clearer later on in this chapter. However, in a time where our curriculum demands more and better problem solving from our students, a way for us to improve our students' problem solving abilities is crucial. Building from this, skill transference also improves where an individual has improved metacognitive abilities. This is again an area that we desperately want our students to improve in. We need our students to be able to draw on learning from other topics and other subjects, and be able to accurately select knowledge and skills to complement different subject areas. Without developing metacognitive skills, this is very, very difficult.

The development of metacognition is also a sure-fire way to improve an individual's self-regulatory abilities. It is perhaps important at this point, to address the misconception that metacognition and self-regulation are the same full. We can think of self-regulation as an umbrella, that includes the regulation of all academic, social, and emotional behaviours. In practice, self-regulation is how an individual controls their emotions and responses across a range of different situations. Metacognition is only a small part of this, where an individual will be controlling their response to an academic task. Therefore, as metacognition is a subset of self-regulation, where metacognitive abilities improve, self-regulation abilities must also improve.

The penultimate benefit of metacognition is that of increased revision effectiveness. We are all too familiar with the students who choose ineffective ways of revising, or focus on the incorrect things to be revising (or perhaps both). Perhaps students choose the easiest topics to revise, or the ones which require the least writing whatever it may be we know that our students are typically not as effective at revising as we would hope. Where individuals have improved metacognitive skills, they are more likely to revise the correct topic areas (that is, areas which are most likely to come up on the assessment or have been accurately identified by the individual as areas that they need to improve), and choose the most effective ways to revise. That is, active revision, not passive.

Which brings us to our final benefit of metacognition: that it complements any other teaching professional development that you are doing. For example, if you are already focussing on modelling, questioning, or feedback, for example, then metacognition can be tied into this. We know that teachers are short for time, and we know that there is never enough time for the reflection and professional development that we are wanting to do. Therefore, the fact that metacognition can dovetail with other areas of focus for schools, like those just mentioned, is a huge benefit, especially for leaders.

The how

Having established a clear rationale for metacognition, we now need to move on to understanding exactly what it is. To begin, we will consider two alternate definitions, one by the American psychologist John H. Flavell, and the other my own.

Flavell wrote in 1976:

> 'I am being metacognitive if I notice that I am having more trouble learning A than B; if it strikes me that I should double check C before accepting it as fact.' (Flavell, 1976, p. 232.)

And I wrote, in 2023:

> '[Metacognition is] the little voice inside your head that constantly evaluates and informs your decisions.' (Burns, 2023, p. 6.)

These definitions focus in on two specific considerations. The first is that metacognition is in relation to cognition. Where there is no cognition, we cannot be metacognitive. Additionally, metacognition is the evaluation of our cognition rather than the fundamental cognitive action or piece of knowledge. The second point of consideration is that the process of metacognition is forever ongoing. Metacognition is the process of planning, monitoring and evaluating our actions, considering what went well and what didn't, considering our specific cognitive knowledge and so much more.

The reason that metacognition can be so hard to understand, is that it is invisible. Whereas cognition and motivation are visible; that is, we can see when a student does a piece of work or completes a physical task, we are not able to see their conscious and subconscious consideration and evaluation of their own cognition. That is, we cannot see their metacognition. It should also probably be noted that metacognitive theory can be quite hard to get your head around. Neither of the above definitions provide us with a perfectly clear understanding of what metacognition actually is. The remainder of this chapter will explore the theory in depth, and so by the end you will have a clear understanding, but this does not take away from the difficulty in wrapping your head around this theory.

Which brings us on nicely to the breakdown of metacognitive theory, our knowledge of cognition, and our regulation of cognition. These two areas, both equally as important as each other (despite the latter area of regulation being far more widely known), are then both themselves split down into three subsequent areas, as shown in the diagram below.

Let us begin with developing our understanding of knowledge of cognition – the part of metacognition which is in relation to how we determine our own levels of knowledge. Instantly, it hopefully appears obvious why this area is just as important as our regulation of cognition. If we are not able to effectively determine what knowledge we do, and do not have, and the approaches that we can take for problems, then we are going to be in a pickle, even if our ability to regulate our cognition is superb.

We begin with an individual's knowledge of task. This refers to an individual's understanding of *exactly* what they need to be doing. This includes things such as time limit, the format that a response or project should be given in, as well as the

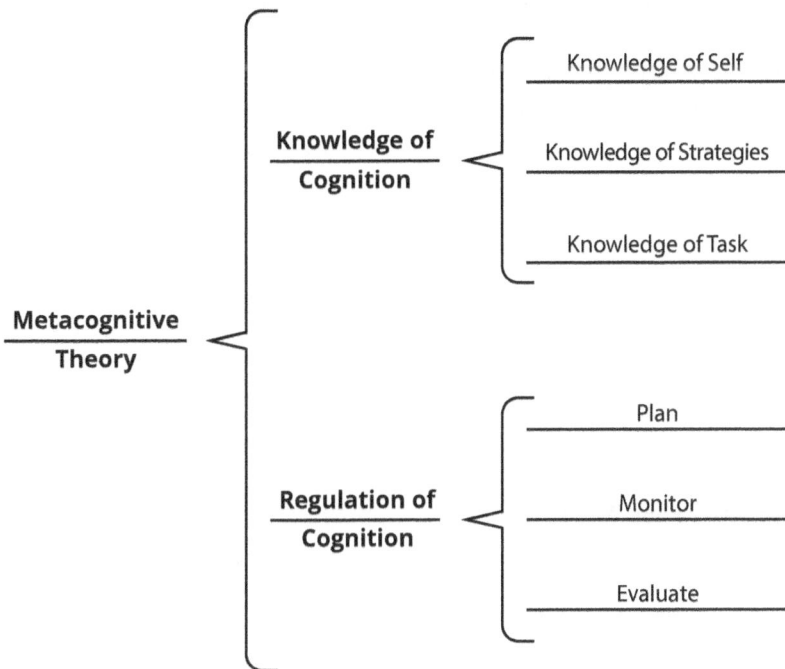

Figure 1.1 Brace map of the six foundations of metacognitive theory

determining success criteria (e.g., 'I need to make six points to get all six marks'). Positively, all students will always have an understanding of task. Negatively, this may not always be an accurate understanding of task. Comprehension is a messy thing, in which all individuals will have their own idea of what it is they ought to be doing, but this can be different to what they really ought to be doing. Without an accurate understanding of task, then an individual will not be producing an effective response to the problem at hand. We therefore have our work cut out, as without an effective knowledge of task, nothing else *really* matters.

Moving on from this, we begin to consider our knowledge of self. This part of metacognition refers to the knowledge that we know that we have, that is relevant for the task at hand, that we can draw upon. The crucial bit here is *knowledge that is relevant*. For example, it is great that a student has swathes of knowledge around elements, bonds and chemical formulas, but if they are unable to select the correct knowledge to answer the question 'define covalent bonding', then their knowledge of self is weak. Individuals need to be able to isolate and effectively determine the relevant knowledge that they have at their disposal for the task at hand.

Thirdly, we come on to an individual's knowledge of strategies. This area of meta-cognition is far more straightforward. Given a task or problem, we typically have more than one way of doing it. Each approach will have its strengths, but also its own weaknesses, and suitability to different problems. This part of metacognition places emphasis on choosing the most appropriate strategy for the task at hand. Where we do not choose the most suitable strategy, we risk anything from taking longer to completing the task than we otherwise would have done, all the way through to not being able to complete the task due to the choice of an ineffective strategy. One example of this area in metacognition would be knowledge of the different types of making a cup of tea (which, at a basic level, could be considering whether to brew the tea straight in a mug or in a teapot).

This is all quite theory heavy, so let us now consider what this would look like for us in our day-to-day jobs. Regardless of the age group that we work with, or the subject that we teach, we will have all had to produce reports for students at some point in time. Let us walk through the knowledge of cognition stages for this process:

Knowledge of Task

- Do I need to write a report for all students, just one particular class, or just one particular subject area?
- Do I need to give written feedback, a grade/score, or both?
- What system am I using to do this?
- How long do I have to do it?
- Do I need to work with any other teachers in order to do this?
- How long is this task going to take to do?
- What does an effective or good report look like?

Knowledge of self

- Do I have all the data that I need in order to write these reports?
- Am I confident with the grade prediction model that the school uses?
- Do I know about personal circumstances which may impact what I say in the report card for some students?
- What do I know about the student who only joined the class three weeks ago?
- Do I know how to use the system that we have been told we must put reports on?

Knowledge of strategies

- Am I going to plan to do all of these reports in one go, or am I going to break them up?
- Would it be better to write in individual statements or should I just use the pre-populated statements on the system?
- Which method of grade prediction should I use?
- Should I cross-reference all of my grades with colleague x?

Having now developed an understanding of knowledge of cognition, we move on to consider regulation of cognition – the more widely known and understood part of metacognitive theory. This area, as shown on the brace map (Figure 1.1), is broken down into planning, monitoring, and evaluation, all far more straightforward areas to understand – obvious, perhaps?

Planning is the approach that a student will take to a task. It may include a consideration of time planning, considering how to go about a task, as well as considering what they need to include in their response. This can sometimes take a written form, but very often will be a mental, and somewhat invisible, process. Intriguingly, effectively planning is typically made up of the three sub-sections of knowledge of cognition. We would often claim that effective planning would include consideration of a task's requirements (knowledge of task), the knowledge that we need to include in it (knowledge of self), as well as the way in which we will approach the task (knowledge of strategies). These metacognitive cycles link together very nicely!

The second part of cognitive regulation is that of monitoring. I like to think of this as the tricky middle bit between planning and evaluation, where we are looking to do some level of immediate evaluation on our progress so far, to ensure that we have the best resulting answer or product. This is difficult, for two reasons. Firstly, monitoring breaks our natural flow state. We need to stop from the 'doing', and instead consider what is going well, if we need to make changes, if we have sufficient time, and so forth. This comes at a time where we typically want to keep our head down and just keep going with the work until we get to the end. This is worse where we are more in a 'flow state'. Secondly, monitoring is especially difficult when we consider the sunk-cost fallacy. This fallacy suggests that where we invest, in effect, blood, sweat, and tears, we will keep going on in the same way, even if we know it is not as efficient as changing tac or even starting again, because, well, because we are human, and human nature is somewhat 'pig-headed'. Despite all of this, the importance of monitoring should not be underestimated, as it means that changes can be made to an individual's work in live time, rather than at the point of evaluation (or even feedback), where it is often too late to make changes to that just completed task.

The final area of consideration is of course evaluation. This is perhaps the most obvious of the three areas, where an individual will consider the task that they have just completed, and review it in relation to the success criteria. Did they include all of the points as required? Did they get the correct final answer? Did they include the required method? Did they manage to finish the task within the time allotted? All of these questions should be asked by the individual of themselves, and the determined responses should, for an effective learner, then be fed back into their future planning, in order to make improvements to their future work. Once again, regulation of cognition is a cycle, where evaluation feeds back to planning, planning feeds into monitoring, and so forth!

Once again, let us now try to contextualise this part of metacognitive theory too, consider the process of planning, delivering, and evaluating a lesson.

Planning
- What is it that I will be teaching students?
- What resources do I need?
- What teaching strategies/approaches am I going to utilise?
- What misconceptions do I need to address?
- Is the seating plan fine as it is?

Monitoring
- Have students understood what they need to?
- Is my use of the TA effective?
- Are students ready to move on to the next task or do they need further support?
- Are my current teaching models effective or do I need to model alternative options?
- Which students do I really need to be working with?

Evaluation
- Did students learn what I needed them to learn?
- Where do I need to begin the next lesson from?
- How would I teach that lesson again?
- What misconceptions arose that I wasn't aware of?
- Do I need to make future changes to the seating plan (etc.)?

Of course, there are a number of additional questions that you would be asking yourself, and numerous other things that you would be planning, but this certainly helps to place some 'meat on the bones' of metacognitive theory.

At this point, metacognitive theory in its entirety has been explored. However, it is worth dwelling on two further points – the myths of metacognition and the fear of implementation.

Firstly, there are some misconceptions around which students that metacognition is suitable for, which I addressed in detail in my first book *Inspiring Deep Learning with Metacognition*. It is worth considering them again though, in case you come up against them while implementing metacognition in your own settings and with your meta-cognitive curriculum work. These myths are:

- Metacognition is only for high-attaining students.
- Metacognition is only for older students.
- Metacognition is not for SEN students.
- Metacognition is better in girls than boys.

You will hopefully see, how through the exploration of the rationale for metacognition earlier on in this chapter, that these are all myths. All students can access metacognitive strategies and develop their metacognitive abilities. Perhaps it is sometimes easier with students who are not struggling with the cognition, and perhaps it is sometimes easier with individuals who have already developed their metacognition further. However, if we do not take the opportunities that we have to improve metacognitive skills in our young people, then they will never actually develop their metacognitive abilities. If we have young people in our classes, then we need to be providing them with opportunities to actively consider, and improve, their metacognitive abilities.

A final point now needs to be made, in reference to previous implementation of metacognition, through the guise of learning to learn in the 2000s and 2010s across UK schools. Typically, this didn't go well, not due to the underlying research base, but the way that it was done. Exactly what went wrong, and how we can avoid that, is explored in the coming chapters, but it is worth addressing that the learning to learn programme, and furthering metacognitive skills in our student and developing a curriculum with opportunity to develop these skills are completely different things. Developing a curriculum, based upon subject specific knowledge, that provides opportunity for metacognitive development through it, is a world away from the learning to learn programme. This may be a concern that you hold, or one that you come up against when making changes in your own educational context.

With the rationale for metacognition established, theory understood, and myths addressed, it is now time for us to consider metacognition and the curriculum. How do we develop it? How do we ensure that it is successful? How do we even decide what we need to focus on? Let us now address these questions.

References

Ben-David, A., and Zohar, A. (2009). Contribution of meta-strategic knowledge to scientific inquiry learning. *International Journal of Science Education, 31*(12), pp. 1657–1682.

Brown, A. L., and DeLoache, J. S. (1978). Skills, plans, and self-regulation. In R. S.Siegler (Ed.), *Children's thinking: What develops?* (pp. 3–35). Hillsdale, NJ: Lawrence Erlbaum.

Burns, N. (2023). *Inspiring Deep Learning With Metacognition: A Guide for Secondary Teaching.* London: SAGE Publications.

Burns, N. (2024). *Teaching Hacks: Fixing Everyday Classroom Issues With Metacognition.* London: SAGE Publications.

Callan, G. L., Marchant, G. J., Finch, W. H., & German, R. L. (2016) Metacognition, strategies, achievement, and demographics: Relationships across countries. *Educational Sciences: Theory and Practice, 16*(5), pp. 1487–1502.

Education Endowment Foundation. (2019). *Metacognition and Self-Regulated Learning: Guidance Report.* London: Education Endowment Foundation.

Flavell, J. H. (1976). Metacognitive aspects of problem solving. In L. B. Resnick (Ed.), *The Nature of Intelligence* (pp. 231–236). Hillsdale, NJ: Erlbaum.

Flavell, J. H., Miller, P. H., & Miller, S. A. (2002). *Cognitive development* (4th ed.). Upper Saddle River, NJ: Prentice Hall.

Kramarski, B., Mevarech, Z. R., & Arami, M. (2002). The effects of metacognitive instruction on solving mathematical authentic tasks. *Educational Studies in Mathematics, 49*(2), pp. 225–250.

Kuhn, D. (1989). Children and adults as intuitive scientists. *Psychological Review, 96*(4), pp. 674–689.

Mevarech, Z. R. (1999). Effects of metacognitive training embedded in cooperative settings on mathematical problem solving. *The Journal of Educational Research, 92*(4), pp. 195–205.

Mevarech, Z. R., and Amrany, C. (2008). Immediate and delayed effects of meta-cognitive instruction on regulation of cognition and mathematics achievement. *Metacognition and Learning, 3*(2), pp. 147–157.

Mevarech, Z. R., and Kramarski, B. (1997). IMPROVE: A multidimensional method for teaching mathematics in heterogeneous classrooms. *American Educational Research Journal, 34*(2), pp. 365–394.

Ofsted. (2019). *Research for the Education Inspection Framework*. London: Ofsted.

Schraw, G. (1998). Promoting general metacognitive awareness. *Instructional Science, 26*(1–2), pp. 113–125.

Teong, S. K. (2003). The effect of metacognitive training on mathematical word-problem solving. *Journal of Computer Assisted Learning, 19*(1), pp. 46–55.

Toth, J. P., Daniels, K. A., & Solinger, L. A. (2000). Age-related differences in the accuracy of judgments of learning: The role of encoding strategies. *Psychology and Aging, 15*(1), pp. 64–75.

Willingham, D. T. (2011). Ask the cognitive scientist: Can teachers increase students' self-control?. *American Educator, 35*(2), pp. 22–27.

Zohar, A., and Ben-David, A. (2008). Explicit teaching of meta-strategic knowledge in authentic classroom situations. *Metacognition and Learning, 3*(1), pp. 59–82.

2

The pitfalls of implementation

Nathan Burns

Introduction

Implementing new pedagogies is a significant undertaking. Firstly, a need has to be identified. What needs to improve? How do you know it is *exactly* that one thing that needs to change? What does the data show, and has it been triangulated with other information? Once the area of need has been identified and interrogated, a solution needs to be determined. Is something going to be removed, tweaked, or added in? What does the research say about possible approaches? How does the context that you are in, along with the other policies that you have, potentially impact the choice of approach that you take? Once determined, an implementation plan needs to be determined. A pre-mortem needs to be run. A timetable of implementation established. A training plan produced.

There are a couple of things for us to consider, from a metacognitive perspective. The first is that you do not really need to go through this process, or at least, in the first instance you do not, anyway. In the same way that we wouldn't question the need to focus on modelling, effective deliberate practice, feedback or behaviour management systems, among many areas, metacognition is also the same. Regardless of the context of your school, the progress that your students are already achieving, and the focus that you have on other areas, such as modelling or questioning, metacognition also fits alongside this. Metacognition is a staple of high-quality teaching. It is not an approach to deal with a progress issue here, or a group of students there. It is a core component of effective teaching, and a key area to develop in each and every one of the students who are in our schools. In short, if you are not already focussing on metacognition, then you need to be. This needs to be a non-negotiable (and if you are in doubt, just refer back to the rationale for metacognition from the first chapter).

The second point to consider is that this is a book regarding metacognition and the curriculum, rather than successful implementation and effective leadership within schools. There are numerous high-quality books, blogs and podcasts which address the process of effective implementation and leadership more generally. At this point, there is nothing that this book can add in to this area of literature where it can add further insight.

However, what this book adds are considerations of implementation from a metacognitive perspective. How we implement changes in schools will vary, of course, by the context that we find ourselves in, but also by the type of approach that we are implementing. This chapter will illuminate how we can go about implementing metacognition in our school contexts successfully, but in a backwards manner. Rather than considering effective implementation, this chapter will focus on what *not* to do, illuminating pitfalls of meta-cognitive implementation, to ensure that you do not fall into them. We begin with a consideration of theory.

The importance of (metacognitive) theory

I am a nerd. I must be, for I am writing a book on the curriculum and metacognition. At the time of writing, I am also completing my Masters on metacognitive leadership, and am planning my PhD, also on metacognition. It is perhaps no surprise that I am invested in educational theory, especially metacognition.

However, I deeply believe that a strong understanding of metacognitive theory is crucial to all members of our staff community if we are going to see metacognitive changes implemented effectively. And by effectively, I mean in a timely manner, without the need for repetitive training (i.e. training repeats, rather than retrieval and further depth training), and, most importantly, in a way that brings about the positive attainment impacts on our students that the literature says that it ought to.

We know, from the first chapter, that metacognitive theory can be quite difficult to get our heads around. Definitions provide an essence of the theory, but not a true understanding. It is only through several thousand words and a few examples that we can really start to grasp when metacognition truly is. In my time speaking at confer-ences and delivering metacognition training in a range of different education contexts, the number of teachers who have spoken to me about their confusion of metacognitive theory, and what it *actually* means, is a significant percentage. This is nothing to be ashamed of – metacognition is invisible, and all too often, not even happening. Addi-tionally, when the word is rarely muttered in our schools, is it any wonder that our teachers are not fully 'clued up' on the theory?

Which means that for us to be successful in embedding metacognition into our schools and our curricula we need our staff to have a very strong understanding of metacognitive theory. Staff need to understand the knowledge and regulation of cognition, and their sub areas. Staff need to understand the key terms, the definitions, and the examples that we have shared, and be able to differentiate between the cognitive action and the metacognitive aspects of those activities.

But why is this so important, beyond the (brief) reasons already mentioned?

1 As you will see later on in this book, when we delve into strategies, you will notice that many of these are not new. Many are tweaks on what we already do, or place emphasis on areas that we may not currently. It is through a strong understanding of metacognitive theory that we understand why these tweaks, or changes in

emphasis, lead to a tool that improves metacognitive abilities in our students. Let us take the example of an exam wrapper, a simple document designed to allow students to evaluate how well they have done after an assessment. This is something straight-forward that happens in a number of schools. This is also a strong metacognitive tool, but not unless changes are made. For example, if an exam wrapper asks the following questions of students:

○   Are you happy with the score you got?
○   Which questions did you get correct?
○   What do you need to work on?

Then we are not really stretching the metacognitive skills of our students. If we truly understand metacognitive theory, we would instead be asking students questions like these:

  Post-completion, but pre-marking:

- What score do you think you will get?
- Which question areas are you confident on, and which are you less confident on?
- Where do you think you will score marks?
- Which question types did you struggle on the most?
- What information or support could have helped you do better in this assessment?
- How long did you revise for in anticipation of this assessment?
- What tools of revision did you use in preparation for this assessment?

Followed by these questions, post-marking:

- How accurate was your score judgement?
- Did you accurately identify the questions that you did get correct and didn't get correct?
- Do you think that the way that you prepared for this exam was effective?
- Were you correct in identifying the types of question(s) that you struggled on?
- What support or information do you *now* think that you may need?
- What areas do you want to highlight for extra support, feedback, or re-teaching?

The list of questions could go on. The point that I am making here, however, is that a better understanding of the theory will support a better understanding of the *essence* that makes something metacognitive. If staff do not quite understand metacognitive theory, emphasis may be placed on the wrong areas (or not at all), and hence the impact will be reduced.

1 Which leads us on to the next important rationale for theory – a teacher's mental model. Effective professional development of course places emphasis on increasing the number of strategies that a teacher has at their disposal. We want teachers to have a vast number of research-backed, and context suitable strategies that they can pull out at a second's notice in order to support the learning of their students. However, the key thing here is not necessarily the strategies (though important),

but actually the mental model of the teacher. We need our teachers to be able to select the strategy that is *most* suitable for the situation that they find themselves in (taking into account a number of factors, but including the content that they are trying to teach, the feedback that they are getting from students, their own experiences and their aim for that period of learning). If teachers are *just* taught about a range of different approaches that they can take in the classroom, this is great, but if they are being used at the wrong times, then this is less good! I firmly believe that a better understanding of metacognitive theory will allow teachers to better select the strategy that most supports the metacognitive development of their students. This is purely logic. A teacher will better select the models that they need to use with students if they better understand a topic and how students themselves learn and develop mental models. This is true of metacognition. A teacher will better select the metacognitive tools at their disposal, if they better understand metacognitive theory themselves and exactly which areas of metacognition (for example, monitoring or evaluation) that they are trying to develop in their own students.

2 Which brings us seamlessly on to lethal mutations. A scary word that is all too often used as a buzzword (and used incorrectly, too). Lethal mutation is the idea that a new approach or strategy is not completely grasped by all of those implementing it. This then means that implementation is different between all of the teachers who have been challenged to implement it. Because of a poorer understanding of this new idea, sometimes this implementation can make the new approach redundant (i.e. there is now no net benefit of this new approach), or, and this is what we really must avoid, this implementation can have a negative impact on our students. This is 'lethal', and hence we must avoid it. There are a number of things that we can do, some of which are explored later in this, and other chapters, but there is one safeguard that we can put in place – a 'pre-mortem', so to speak. Through ensuring that staff have a strong understanding of metacognition more generally, then, independently, be more able to determine if their implementation is in line with the theory. If teachers truly understand what metacognition is, and what they are aiming to do with their metacognitive implementation, then they are far less likely to implement it badly.

3 The next benefit of strong metacognitive understanding in our staff body is to avoid of the 'jingle jangle' fallacy. For effective implementation, as defined above, we need to ensure that the following do not occur:

a Jingle – two teachers, departments, or leaders are naming something the same, but are actually talking about two different things.

b Jangle – two teachers, departments, or leaders are really talking about the same idea but giving it two different names.

   Both of these scenarios are ones that we want to avoid. The jingle scenario means that we are going to be having two individuals comparing 'apples and pears', and trying to discuss, for example, how they each use the strategy and what goes well, and what they need to improve on, but any subsequent conclusions are somewhat invalidated by the fact that they are talking about different things! The jangle scenario will mean that two individuals won't realise that they are talking about the same thing, risking confusion and ineffective conversations. Through ensuring both effective metacognitive training of our staff, and a consistent vocabulary around the key terminology and strategies that we are using (this latter point is raised later on in this book, too), we safeguard ourselves against the jingle jangle fallacy and again, support the likelihood of effective implementation.

4 A key point that Mary Myatt addresses in her book *The Curriculum: Gallimaufry to Coherence* (Myatt, 2018), is around the importance of subject knowledge. Myatt suggests that where subject knowledge is poor, it is far harder to deliver a lesson of the highest quality. Myatt goes on to provide a useful analogy – that of a restaurant. Imagine a perfect atmosphere, beautiful decor, superb waiting staff, but then, horrific food, where the chef is just not all that good. If the chef can't cook, then the whole restaurant experience is ruined. In the classroom, if the teacher does not understand the content, the lesson would be poor. The same is true of metacognition. If the teacher does not understand what metacognition is, then they are unlikely to be able to deliver it in a successful manner.

Don't forget the cognition

There is one significant difference with metacognitive implementation and most other educational approaches. The need to embed it within cognition.

One thing that has yet to be mentioned in this book is why the link between metacognition and curriculum? Surely a book of strategies, or a book developing a teacher's mental model as to when to best use these strategies would be more effective? No. Let us consider what metacognition truly is – the consistent reflection upon, and regulation of, our cognition. Metacognition only exists where there is cognition. No cognition, no metacognition. The most cognitively demanding part of schools is of course the curriculum. It is the vehicle through which we establish what, how and when we are going to teach our students. Therefore, it is through the curriculum that we must embed metacognition. Just as Jim Carville said in 1992, 'it's the cognition, stupid'. (He of course didn't say this, but had he been talking about metacognition rather than the economic state of the US, then I am sure he would have done...)

To break this down further, let us consider the following four points:

1 Metacognitive development must be within the context of content
2 Metacognition must be developed across the wider curriculum
3 Metacognition is not a bolt-on or just an enrichment opportunity
4 Metacognition should not be taught as a discrete lesson

Understanding metacognitive theory, statement (1) is clear. Where there is no cognition occurring, then metacognition cannot occur. We ought to avoid trying to develop metacognition in the absence of subject specific teaching, and so, metacognition and the curriculum are natural bedfellows.

We must also avoid metacognitive strategies being used inconsistently. Too often, and especially with new approaches, initial high use quickly peters out, and any benefit that could have been seen through established a new approach long-term, is lost. This is all a situation that we have seen in schools in which we have worked. Considering that metacognition must be tied to cognition (or, for the remainder of this book, I will say curriculum), it makes sense that to ensure its successful implementation, that suitable (metacognitive) strategies are chosen, and built in across the curriculum. This ensures that these strategies are used on a frequent basis (and this is not to say that they should be used once a week, every (Metacognitive) Monday or such like, but rather in line with suitability), and hence become embedded and their power realised. Where these strategies are only considered by teachers as new approaches in the classroom, it is very easy for them to become forgotten within a few weeks as other demands, pressures and priorities take over. Tying together metacognition and the curriculum, across all of your subjects and year groups, will ensure that this does not happen.

But point (2) can often make metacognition feel like a bolt-on, or enrichment activity. If strategies need to be frequently used in the classroom, it would be easy to offer them as a stretch challenge for students who are done, or for students who find the work too easy. Ignoring the points around the efficacy of stretch and challenge, and the need for a goldilocks level of difficult in work, we do need to make sure that metacognition is not only built into the curriculum (as above) but also built in at appropriate times. The reason for this latter half of this book, exploring metacognition in a range of subject specialisms, if for exactly this reason. Through identifying the areas where different, effective, metacognitive strategies can be used, it can be ensured that these strategies become integrated with the cognitive elements of the lesson. This is where metacognition truly develops, hand in hand with cognitive considerations. And so, where metacognitive approaches are embedded not just within the curriculum, but hand-in-hand with units and topics, we see them being used at appropriate times, in a manner that really supports the metacognitive development of our students.

Finally, we come to the teaching of metacognition as a discrete lesson. The concerns around the old Learning to Learn programme should be sufficient in putting you off, but there is always the feeling that we ought to be doing more. Could we perhaps teach some of these metacognitive strategies through tutor time, so that students are aware of them before they come up in their subject lessons? In short, no. If you want to successfully implement metacognition within your classrooms, then do not try and rush in this way. Ensure that the development of metacognitive strategies is within the curriculum and tied in to cognitive thought.

Consider the cognitive load

Despite the concern with teaching metacognitive strategies outside of the curriculum, we do of course need to teach the strategies at some point. Surely the answer, as I stated above, is that these metacognitive strategies and development happens within the confines of the subject classroom, right? Yes. But there is more that we need to consider, and it begins with cognitive load.

We are all likely to be familiar with cognitive load by now. In short, and simplified for the purposes of the explanation I am about to make, cognitive load is the amount of information that we can deal with in our working memory at any given time. Imagine a pint glass, representing our working memory capacity, and water, representing the content being poured in (either new content that we are attending to, or recalled information from our long-term memory). If we just keep pouring into the glass, it will quickly overflow. This is exactly what happens to our working memory if we try and attend to too much information at once. The implications of this for metacognition are huge and need to be understood if metacognition is going to be develop effectively within our curriculum and across our schools.

As highlighted, metacognitive strategies are going to need to be taught. Students are going to need to be shown how to use a new graphic organiser, how to complete an exam wrapper, or shown how to plan out their revision using the Leitner flash card method, for example. All of these methods, should, as highlighted, be developed with students within the context of content, to ensure that they make more sense. But we need to consider the cognitive load of doing this. If we are trying to teach students a new metacognitive strategy, but we are also doing it with new cognitive knowledge and skills, then this is likely to lead to overload. The cognitive action will not have been learnt, and the metacognitive skill will not have been understood. This scenario needs to be avoided, and hence there are two rules that we can consider for effective meta-cognitive teaching:

New curriculum + Known metacognitive strategy

Known curriculum + New metacognitive strategy

Through ensuring that one of the inputs that our students are attending to is from our long-term memory, we are ensuring that there is more space in our 'pint glass' for the new knowledge to fill. If we are able to link together new cognitive knowledge with a known metacognitive strategy, or the other way around, we are putting ourselves in a far better place to be able to master both.

This may seem simple, but it is not always so. Let us draw back to the exam wrapper from far earlier in this chapter. If we utilised the metacognitive essence wrapper (the second example), there is a lot of information that is new to students; a significant amount of in-depth consideration would need to occur. If this is in relation to a new assessment, students may struggle to both understand exactly how to use the wrapper effectively *and* effectively consider the assessment that they have just done. We have some solutions, therefore, in considering how we would deliver this activity.

1 Pre-teach the use of the wrapper using an old assessment. This is unlikely to help the student to illuminate any new understanding from that assessment, but it does instead mean that they can just focus on 'getting their head around' the wrapper.
2 Model each question of the wrapper, so students are only having to deal with one question at a time.
3 Begin with the second part of the wrapper, after students have already received their mark, and build up the number of questions, and hence quantity and depth of reflection, that students are having to do.

In summary, when developing the metacognitive curriculum, consideration will need to be given to the implementation of strategies in the classroom. This may be through training, faculty meetings, or in-depth unit plans. It is also for this reason why strategy consistency across all subject areas can be helpful. Not only do we want to avoid the jingle jangle fallacy, but we also want students to develop a strong understanding of a select group of metacognitive strategies quickly (and thus cement them into long-term memory), allowing new cognition to be considered in relation to them, rather than students having a very surface level understanding of a vast number of metacognitive approaches. Through consistent strategy use across subject areas, the former is far more likely to happen.

Time

Which brings us to time. Oh, time! How we wish we had more. Our time is limited, and the amount of time that we can direct towards metacognitive development is perhaps limited. Therefore, what do we really need to consider?

The first consideration is that the curriculum is *never* finished. Unlike other interventions, such as timetable changes or the restructuring of Physical, Social, Health, and Economic (PSHE) education, developmental aims, such as curriculum improvement, have success criteria, but no real end point. Constant improvement can, and should be made. Therefore, if we are looking to incorporate metacognition into the curriculum, then we need to be aware, and comfortable, with the idea that we will never be *done*. However, this is not to say that we will not have success criteria, goals and deadlines for certain parts of development. Rather, it is to say that we will constantly need to reflect on which metacognitive aspects we are focussing on, where we are embedding them, and how they are going, in order to consistently improve on our previous implementation. In effect, we need to be metacognitive about our metacognitive development.

The second consideration is that metacognitive curriculum development needs to be subject specific. What metacognition looks like in one area is likely to look slightly different in another, because it is related to the cognition that is being drawn upon and developed. Due to this, a whole school aim of metacognitive development may be established, but this does not mean that each subject area is going to develop at the same rate. There are many factors for this, which can be as complicated as staff turnover and a need to focus on alternative priorities (such as behaviour management), or less complicated in that the department has not been as successful as it had hoped with its implementation at first, so is making changes to improve this. Each faculty area will need support, through their line manager and specific training and support, and each faculty area will also need to be held to account for any deadlines set. However, development across all areas is not going to be consistent, nor at a consistent rate.

Thirdly, metacognitive development is not a one term, or even one year, aim. As should be clear from this book so far is that metacognition needs to be deeply embedded within the curriculum, and then teased out and developed in our students through high-quality teaching, delivered by practitioners who are confident in their under-standing of metacognitive theory. This is not going to happen overnight. Rather, I would implore every school who is looking at making these changes to begin with a five-year metacognition development plan and then work backwards from this. Exactly how you will do this is determined in the next chapter, but the key takeaway here is that effective metacognitive change that becomes sustained and embedded takes time. As Howard and Hill (2020) wrote, we must avoid hurried implementation with the cur-riculum, ensuring that we carve out time for training and implementation. This is not a one-term journey.

References

Howard, K., and Hill, C. (2020). *Symbiosis: The Curriculum and the Classroom*. Melton: John Catt Educational.

Myatt, M. (2018). *The Curriculum: Gallimaufry to Coherence*. Melton: John Catt Educational.

3

Determining your focus

Nathan Burns

Introduction

You have decided that you want to develop metacognition in your school, and curriculum is the vehicle to develop this. However, it isn't just as simple as saying 'let's embed metacognition!', even where you have conducted a pre-mortem, including the factors identified in the previous chapter. As detailed, metacognitive development in schools needs to be a long-term project, implemented over the course of several years. Despite this, you still need to establish a starting point for your implementation. There are two areas of consideration; the area of metacognitive development, and the current metacognitive abilities of students.

Determining metacognitive levels of students

There are a couple of strong reasons to consider the current metacognitive levels of students. The first is as a point of reference for any interventions and changes to the curriculum. It is always helpful to be able to measure the impact that changes have, and by taking a baseline of student's metacognitive abilities, you are better able to do this. The second reason to determine the levels of students is to ensure that the correct metacognitive strategies are being introduced. Pitch the metacognitive strategies too low, and the benefits will be minimal, but pitch them too high and the benefits won't be earned that way, either. It's all about the goldilocks level of challenge, once again.

How do you go about measuring the levels of metacognitive abilities in students, though? Once again, there are a couple of ways of going about doing this, with one being suitably more straightforward than the other.

The first way is through using the work of Perkins (1992), that describes the four different levels of metacognitive learner (because unfortunately for us, metacognitive abilities are neither on or off). The four levels are tacit, aware, strategic, and reflective.

1 Tacit

An individual is not actively aware that they are in control of their cognitive processes, and thus would not take the time to consider the best approaches that they can take for tasks, or how the feedback that they have just received should inform their future work, for example. In this scenario, we are most likely just trying to get the student to actively, rather than passively, engage with the cognitive task at hand, rather than anything deeper.

- A tacit student may:
- Be unable to explain the steps that they have just worked through
- Be unable to communicate the cognitive processes that they have drawn upon
- Struggle to apply their cognition to a new context
- Struggle to infer content beyond any given model
- Not determine steps for improvement following a given task
- Not act upon any given feedback

2 Aware

An aware individual is conscious that they could be making different cognitive decisions, for example using one strategy rather than another, or planning out their response in a slightly different way. However, an aware learner does not act upon this thinking. They know that they could make changes, but they don't actually do anything about it. For want of a better term, this is a very passive metacognitive individual.

An aware student may:

- Be able to explain the stages that they went through
- Engage at a very simple level to planning or reflection questions (such as 'next time I'll re-read' – a fairly vague statement)
- At times show that they are planning and evaluating their work
- Engage inconsistently with feedback to push forward their own learning
- Need 'spoon feeding' next steps for improvement
- Appear very passive in pushing forward their own learning
- Have difficulty explaining *why* they have done certain things, but could communicate the process

3 Strategic

A student who is strategic is not only aware of the cognitive choices that they are making, but now does act upon them. They consciously plan how they are going to approach tasks, carefully considering their knowledge of the task, their knowledge of self and the variety of ways in which they can complete the task. Equally, this type of individual is also reflective, considering what went well, and what did not, as well as how they will make changes in future. They will also take on board feedback to improve future outcomes.

- A strategic learner is likely to:
- Consistently plan out approaches to their work and evaluate what could have gone better and what went well, without input
- Act upon feedback given by an expert (i.e. a teacher)
- Be more independent in driving forward their own learning and development

- ○ Engage with learning objectives and success criteria in order to identify areas for improvement
- ○ Ask for support and guidance in identifying how they can improve
- ○ Far more conscientious about improving their own work
- ○ Will be better able to communicate why they have done certain things

4 Reflective

The only difference between a strategic individual and one who is reflective is that the latter individual will also monitor their work while they are completing it. Monitoring, that tricky middle bit where you try and evaluate how you are doing, as you are doing it, if done well, is likely to lead to an improved outcome versus those who are not monitoring. The reflective individual will do this, as well as everything that the strategic individual is doing.

- ○ A reflective individual will consistently:
- ○ Display the characteristics of a strategic learner
- ○ Monitor their work as they go along
- ○ Ask and self-check work as they progress
- ○ Identify gaps as they move along and look for immediate support or identify scaffolds to self-support
- ○ Continue to plan, monitor, and evaluate even where there is not a knowledge other available to discuss any conclusions or to ask questions of (for example, when revising at home or completing homework tasks).
- ○ Seek to go above and beyond to improve their performance

Overall, the type of learner that we are likely to have in our classrooms is one who is either metacognitively tacit, or metacognitively aware. We will have some students who are strategic too, and the odd one or two here and there who we are confident are reflective, but my experiences working with a number of schools in different contexts are that students lie in those first two categories. It isn't really a surprise either. If we aren't developing metacognition through the curriculum, then students would not naturally improve their metacognitive skills. It is only where heed is paid to developing metacognitive skills that those skills do actually start to improve.

Considering this, how can we use this as a measure to judge the metacognitive progress of our students. There are again, a few different routes that we could consider, which include:

- Determining a metacognitive level for every single student, based upon these four levels, as outlined by Perkins, that encompasses all subject areas.
- Determining a metacognitive level for every single student, based upon these four levels as outlined by Perkins, in each subject area.
- Rank students in a comparative judgement process, determining the most metacognitive student down to the least metacognitive student, and thus determining groupings of students who show the characteristics of each of the four levels that Perkins outlined.

There is one further option too, and it is the one I would suggest that you use. The above three options all have one problem in common – they are very long-winded. The staff time judging metacognitive levels using these methods would be large, and this time could be better spent actually considering how metacognition could be developed within the classroom. What we do not need to start doing is reporting a metacognitive level against each student, like some sort of report score, so there isn't the need to go into the depth of those options. Rather, I would propose that judgements are made for a subject area, or year group as a whole, utilising data that we already have, and consistently collect. This means using learning walk data, book looks, other instruments of quality assurance, as well as staff and student voice.

In order to measure in this way effectively, a clear understanding of these levels would be needed. Providing staff with examples of what they would see or hear from students would also be helpful, to bring these levels to 'life' – for example, by sharing the above bullet points. However, once staff are clear on these different levels of metacognition, it would be very easy to determine what levels a typical subject area or year group are working at, in order to provide that base layer for judgement. It also means that metacognition can be included within quality assurance more easily. Noted, this should not be for judgement purposes, but to track improvements for students and to determine high-quality practices around school which can be shared across the staff body. Staff may, eventually, hold a performance management target to introduce or refine a metacognitive approach in the classroom, but an unfair target would be for students to move from one metacognitive level to another (so don't think about going down this path, either!).

As outlined above, there is also a more in-depth measure of metacognition, through the form of a short assessment. Effective measures of metacognitive abilities are few and far between. Confusions in the definitions of metacognition (and conflation with self-regulation), as well as contextual differences, mean that many of the test measures available are inconsistent. The benefit of having some sort of test, and hence a numerical score, is of course to have a quicker and more accurate way of judging metacognitive improvement. If you did want to go down this route, I would recommend using the Junior Metacognitive Awareness Inventory (Jnr MAI) as the tool to do this. A short, but true to the literature test, the Jnr MAI is comparatively quick to administer (questions could be put into a short Google Forms for students to complete, for example) and does provide a numerical score. Something to consider if you do decide to go down this route!

But where to begin?

Whether or not you decide to determine the metacognitive starting point of students, you will need to determine exactly where to start with the metacognitive changes to your curriculum. The foci that you determine, is crucial. Fortunately, there isn't really a wrong answer here, but rather a few different options, which will suit different schools at different times.

If you did begin this process through either an in-depth or surface level analysis of the metacognitive skills of students, this may have shone a light on the metacognitive areas that you would like to focus on first. Later in the book, where subject specialists write about what metacognition looks like in their discipline area, they refer back to three different areas – planning, monitoring and evaluation – in keeping with that regulation of cognition cycle. Therefore, does your analysis show that any of the areas in particular are weak for students, and hence ought to be an initial focus for development? If, perhaps, there is no clear area that students need to work on first, then choosing one strategy from each of those three areas, to ensure that they each have the opportunity to developing equally, would be a good choice.

Another option to determine a focus is to consider which pedagogical areas that you already have as a focus within school. Perhaps the current aim for the year is to develop teacher modelling, or perhaps it is to improve oracy in the classroom? Where possible, if metacognitive developments can be aligned with other whole school priorities, then this is advantageous. Though the strategies detailed later on in the book are broken down into the areas of planning, monitoring, and evaluation, it is clear that some of these strategies will need to be teacher led (planning), some will require student response (questioning or feedback), while others require more discussion in the classroom (oracy). Therefore, whatever your main school focus is, you will be able to determine which of the metacognitive strategies align to this, and potentially place a focus on them. In essence, it is possible to choose strategies which help you to tackle a tame problem, such as 'modelling to students is not as in-depth as it could be', and complement the current approach that you are taking, rather than adding in a whole different tranche of approaches.

A third option is to determine the wicked problems that you face in school. There are of course numerous wicked problems, and one establishment's tricky problem is another tame problem. However, these types of problems may include:

- Students are not sufficiently independent
- Homework completion rates are poor
- Students are ineffective when they are revising
- Engagement with problem solving is poor
- Students lack strong comprehension skills
- Students struggle with longer form writing skills
- Students lack a positive learner identity

Though the strategies given in this book are not clearly directed towards solving these different problems, each of them can help to provide part of the solution to one of these problems. For example, the modelling strategy 'problem-solving grids' would support students in improving their engagement with problem solving, while 'wrappers' can have the potential to improve an individual's self-learner identity and to improve the efficiency of future revision. Wicked problems, like those outlined, do not have simple solutions, nor do they have a playbook that we are able to follow. Rather, we need numerous different approaches, to tackle the problem from a number of angles, where the full staff body are on board. These metacognitive approaches can help us here, too.

Fewer things, greater depth

Having determined an area to focus on, it is easy to fall into the trap of choosing to implement every strategy presented that fits into that category. If they all support the development of that area, then we ought to implement them all, right? No. Wrong. Rather, the aim with developing metacognition is to do fewer things, but to do them with greater depth.

Determining exactly which strategies are going to be implemented is addressed further in chapter 5, where a consideration of whole-school priorities and subject specialisms is considered. However, it is crucial that when determining a focus, we are clear that this does not mean that a significant number of strategies need to be implemented at any one time.

A rule of thumb that I often use when implementing metacognitive strategies into the class is to introduce up to two new strategies to any given class, and where possible, limit the number of new metacognitive strategies being unveiled across the whole school to three at a time. Additionally, I would urge these strategies to be implemented across the whole school year, or at worst, across two terms. It would be a huge stretch to introduce two new ideas per term, and hence six per year, without stretching staff, overloading students, or risking poor implementation.

Therefore, an average of one new strategy per term feel suitable. It is here where depth is important. A metacognitive strategy has not been embedded if it crops up in a few lessons, gets ticked off during some learning walks, and a handful of students in student voice can pay a strategy some lip-service when asked about it. An analogy to consider here is learning versus performance. Recalling a fact for a few days or even few weeks does not mean something is learnt. New information is learnt when it is safely transferred to our long-term memory, and it sits within our wider mental model, activated as required, and can be utilised in conjuncture with other skills and knowledge that we have. A metacognitive strategy becomes embedded when it is used consistently, throughout the whole curriculum (rather than just a given unit at the start of the year), and is used freely, independently, and without scaffold, by students. It should be part of the natural delivery of a lesson, and shouldn't appear awkward, performative or a bolt-on. Equally, we can only truly say that a metacognitive strategy is embedded within the curriculum where we have been through a few iterations of the strategy, understanding exactly when it is, and is not suitable, to use within a subject discipline, and refine the utilisation of the strategy.

Therefore, however tempting it is to bring a number of strategies to the fore as soon as a focus area is identified, this is unwise. Effective metacognitive development occurs where it is embedded within the curriculum, and this isn't going to happen where a plethora of strategies get introduced at the start of each INSET day.

Having a strategy journey

Just because it is unwise to introduce a number of new strategies at just one point, that does not mean that it is unwise to have a plan for when other, different strategies, that complement the work that you are doing, can be implemented. Far from it in fact!

Having determined your foci, and identified the strategies that you want to implement, it is then wise to consider what order you want to implement them in. This is where it can be helpful to have an understand of the current metacognitive level of students, ensuring that you are choosing the correct strategy for where students are right now. However, even if you don't have this information, you are unlikely to go wrong!

Utilising the principal stated above, of an average of one new strategy per term, it would be wise to make a plan across several years, to determine what strategies are going to be implemented at what point. What are your priority strategies to implement next term? In this academic year? And hence, what is the priority for year 2, year 3 and so forth. For example:

Year 1, Term 1 – Strategy A
Year 1, Term 2 – Strategy B
Year 1, Term 3 – Strategy C
Year 2, Term 1 – Strategy D
Year 2, Term 2 – Strategy E

You get the point here! The ordering is up to you, but as long as it in conscious of the theory and the miss-steps that can occur, as detailed in the first two chapters, you will likely be on the path to success.

Depending on your establishment, you may have a 5- or 7-year plan, depending on how many school years you cater for. Again, it would be wise to track a journey that is equivalent in length to the number of school years that you cater for. Metacognitive embedding is not an overnight job, and so aligning your long-term plan with the length of time a student will be in your school for, makes sense. This also allows you to build up your strategies. Some strategies build nicely into each other – for example, process questioning builds into the use of the Knowledge of Grid strategy, and thus, sequencing them in such a way could be helpful. However, and to alleviate worry, the sequencing of metacognitive strategies is unlikely to improve metacognitive development at any greater rate, it is simply to support the effective implementation of such strategies.

There is one problem, however, for which this book does not have a perfect answer. If you begin your metacognitive journey at the start of a school year, by the time that your next cohort of students is starting the school, you will be moving on to implementing strategy 4, (if you use the rough template given above). This is fine for all cohorts who were at the school from the start of the previous year, but for the new cohort of students, are they expected to learn how to use this fourth strategy, and also pick up on the previous three some sort of wizardry or specialist absorption techniques? This seems a tad unlikely. There are two sensible approaches that can be taken.

1 The first three strategies are embedded within the curriculum are embedded in the curriculum of all year groups. The second three strategies are embedded within the curriculum of all year groups, bar the youngest year. The next three strategies are embedded within the curriculum of all year groups, bar the two youngest years. And so forth. You would end up with curriculums that looked a little like this:

Reception/Year 7 – Strategy 1, 2 and 3
Year 1/Year 8 – Strategy 1, 2, 3, 4, 5 and 6
Year 2/Year 9 – Strategy 1, 2, 3, 4, 5, 6, 7, 8 and 9
And so on and so forth.

You may, in the end, not implement more than five strategies, which, at a push, can be implemented within a year, meaning any new cohort can be up to speed with these metacognitive strategies by the end of their first year with you. Where you use further strategies, a plan like this, in somewhat amended form, I'm sure, can be utilised, in order to develop the metacognitive skills of students as they progress up the years with you. In some respects, a metacognitive curriculum itself is being developed (but not outside of the subject curriculum itself, crucially), so that students have a clear metacognitive development journey upon which they travel. This is another reason why having some level of sequence and build to the metacognitive strategies that you implement can be nice (but again, not crucial).

2 The second approach that you can take is that all students, regardless of the year that they are in, and when they joined the school, use all of the strategies that teachers have painstakingly developed and embedded into the curriculum. For students in the school from day dot, this isn't so much of an issue. For students new to the school, it is, but a solution for this is explored below. The benefit of this approach is that all students can benefit instantly from all metacognitive strategies, while ensuring that teachers have the greatest range of metacognitive strategies available to them to draw upon in the curriculum that they are delivering, allowing staff to choose the most appropriate strategy for the work that they are doing (and not being hamstrung by the strategies that the year group have developed, as may occur with the first approach).

What does success look like?

The final part of this chapter links us back to the first – judging success. If you began by making metacognitive judgements of students, then this part is easy. New data gets compared to old data, and boom, a judgement can be made, right? But perhaps success is something deeper than that? Perhaps success is having the metacognitive strategies that you determined as priorities to be embedded within your school. What, therefore, does success look like? The following will be strong measures of whether metacognition has been successfully embedded.

- There is high fidelity in the implementation of strategies within and across faculty areas.

- The choice and use of metacognitive strategies complements the uniqueness of each subject areas, rather than limiting or even hindering it (i.e. it should not be shoe-horned in).
- Lethal mutation has been avoided and active ingredients of implementation are clear to see.
- Staff are able to accurately recall what metacognition is, the strategy that they are using, why they are using them, and how they are implementing them effectively in the classroom.
- Students are actively using metacognitive strategies without the (consistent) need for them to be scaffolded.
- Metacognitive strategies are clearly outlined within the curriculum of all subject areas *and*
- Are utilised within lessons as the curriculum described.
- Where metacognitive strategies can be explained by students, and are actively evidenced as being used within their work.
- Metacognition is clearly evidence through learning walks and is not delivered performatively.
- Metacognitive best practice and further discussion continues to be a fundamental of staff meetings both whole school and subject specific.

There are likely other factors that can be considered too – but the priority ought not be a score on a mark book somewhere. This would tell us that these strategies are working, but so would all of these other factors too. Instead, consider a triangulated and more dialogical approach to the consideration of effective embedding of new approaches. As Tom Sherrington (2019) wrote, we need to 'give maximum value to the process, not the products', which complements the thoughts of Christine Counsell (In 'The Curriculum', 2020), who wrote that the curriculum should not be seen as a set of progress levels, but rather a progression model. Instead, curriculum should be judged as a continuous cycle of iteration and reflection (Ashbee, 2021).

References

Ashbee, R. (2021). *Curriculum: Theory, Culture and the Subject Specialisms*. London: Routledge.

Counsell C. (2020). The curriculum. In Sealy, C. (Ed.), *The researchED Guide to The Curriculum: An Evidence-Informed Guide for Teachers*. Woodbridge: John Catt Educational.

Perkins, D. (1992). *Smart Schools: From Training Memories to Educating Minds*. New York: Free Press.

Sherrington, T. [@teacherhead] (2019, June 7). *A Plea to School Leaders Around Curriculum Review: Give Maximum Value to the Process, Not the Products*. [Post]. X. Available at: https://x.com/teacherhead/status/1137007198108889088

4

Embedding change

Nathan Burns

Introduction

Change is surely only successful should that change be determined as positive, for both students and staff alike, but also if that positive change has been embedded and sustained moving forwards. Far too often, changes can be made in an area while it remains a priority, but as soon as the focus switches to a different area, the positive gains in the original area begin to be forgotten as attention is directed elsewhere. Equally, where staff turnover occurs, a loss of knowledge and understanding of these positive changes is also likely to occur. Additionally, where nationally mandated changes in education occur, as they do oh so often in our area of focus, the curriculum, new requirements can squeeze out previously hard-fought positive advancements in what we were already doing.

This chapter is going to explore factors pertinent to embedding metacognitive changes, across faculties and a whole-school, and how we can ensure that these changes remain positive, embedded and sustained.

The long-term lens

Utilising a long-term plan, and considerations around the time requirements that effective metacognitive implementation will need have been key themes in the previous two chapters. Metacognitive changes are not going to happen overnight. Having metacognition as a focus for only one school year will not bring about the greatest possible positive impact of curricula changes, nor will it allow for the embedding and sustaining of positive changes. It is imperative to firstly idealise the 'perfect' metacognitive school, and curriculum:

- What strategies are teachers going to be using, and why?
- What strategies are students going to be familiar with, and when we will they use them?
- What do independent and resilient learners do consistently?
- Where is metacognition consistently been recorded in the curriculum?
- How has the metacognitive approach within the curriculum been refined?
- What common language will staff and students be using around school?

Having identified the key factors of success, staging posts for progress during academic years can be determined. Success should not be as reductive as determining a quantity of strategies that staff should be using in their lessons, but rather, something far deeper. Considerations of application within the curriculum, adaptation and revision of met-acognitive approaches, student voice and parent/carer feedback, as well as continued whole-staff feedback and evidence from learning walks all provide suitable year-end targets to ensure sustained implementation.

It should however be noted that metacognition does not need to be the *one* focus that a department or school has across the course of five years. Many areas will need to be worked on across this time, and metacognition does not provide a fix for every problem that a school faces. It would be churlish to suggest otherwise. What metacognition does provide us with, however, is a lens through which we can view and tackle problems. Perhaps during one academic year, modelling becomes a key focus, or perhaps it is questioning, developing independent learners or tackling low levels of student resilience. Each of these areas can be viewed with a metacognitive lens, and thus, metacognition can remain a key part of school improvement, without being the only area of consideration. Entwining school development areas with a metacognition 'vine' ensures that metacognition continues to be focused upon, continues to be reviewed, adapted, and kept at the forefront of minds, for teachers and students alike, but it does not become all-consuming, failing to allow for other crucial of areas in Teaching and Learning to have a spotlight shone upon them. As Mary Myatt (2018, p. 16) wrote, 'it is never going to be possible to do it all'!

Active ingredients

One key feature of the EEF's first report on effective implementation in schools (Sharples et al., 2018) was around the idea of active ingredients. This concept allows us to isolate the key criteria that will make the implementation of a new approach successful, and hence the need for these aspects to be displayed by all teachers, at all stages of their careers, and in all lessons, with all students. This concept of active ingredients allows us to capture the *essence* of a teaching approach, and understand the foundation that make it so. By isolating these foundations, or 'capturing the essence' of an approach, we can provide staff with the core aspects that must be displayed within a lesson, planning, feedback and so forth.

An effective way of determining this is through utilising that long-term lens, as explored above. Through idealisation of the perfect metacognitive school and curriculum, we work backwards to determine stage posts of progress at the end of each academic year on this journey. Once these progress markers have been determined, active ingredients can be easier to capture. If, for example, a target for the end of the first year of implementation is that common language is used around planning (knowledge of task, knowledge of self, and knowledge of strategies), a key ingredient for success would be that this becomes the new language for planning within school, by all teachers, in all subjects. Evidencing this would be through book work, dialogical quality assurance of lessons, professional development conversations, and student voice, for example (as well as a marked improvement in student planning abilities).

Where active ingredients, or commonly required language and approaches, are not mandated, we end up with the possibility of inconsistent, and potentially poor, implementation. Furthermore, if a whole-school teaching policy does not have commonly understood, agreed and practiced approaches, the inconsistency of this will mean that embedding and sustaining this change would not be possible. We would, in effect, be baking in inconsistencies to our teaching approach. Thus, through the establishment of active ingredients, a considerate subject discipline approach, and effective teaching, consistent approaches can be baked in. Additionally, this allows for easier amalgamation of teaching approach for new members of staff, who can develop their approach in line with the consistent approach displayed by all other members of staff. Howard and Hill (2020) detailed how this type of approach can support less experienced and novice teachers, and help to future proof future curriculum delivery.

Austin's butterfly

Perhaps the most overused analogy in curriculum development is Austin's Butterfly. You'll know the one. A student sketches out their own interpretation of a butterfly, which is simplistic in its construction. Through a process of teacher feedback and student revision, the butterfly improves stage-upon-stage, resulting, at the sixth attempt, the most beautifully drawn and coloured butterfly.

This process of attempt, feedback and revise is a learning technique as old as time, but one as equally adept at explaining the transformation that our curriculum takes. The first draft of a curriculum is no more than a skeleton upon which we will build from, much like the first draft of the butterfly. That initial draft resembles a curriculum (or a butterfly), that first draft is limited in its depth, quality and refinement. This is perfectly natural. No good curriculum will be done in just one draft.

I believe that it is now more widely understood that a curriculum goes through many iterations, and that actually, a curriculum is never *done*. It can be closer to completion, and the revisions required to it are reduced term-upon-term and year-upon-year, but it is never actually *finished*. This frame of thinking is required when we consider the meta-cognitive alternations that we are making to our curriculum.

Given that the curriculum is the vehicle that allows the greatest possible chance for effective metacognitive implementation, we must understand that the changes that we make will, initially resemble that basic butterfly. It will be clear that opportunities for metacognition have been identified in the curriculum, and appropriate strategies have been chosen, but perhaps no more than that. Through professional conversations, observations, and actual teaching, an understanding of how best to use these strategies, and exactly when they should be used, will be determined. As strategies are used more frequently, they will be delivered more effectively, stimulate greater and deeper thinking, and at consistently more appropriate times within the curriculum. As teaching, and professional conversations continue, alternations to metacognition in the curriculum will occur, and gradually the butterfly, that is metacognition within the curriculum, will begin to become deeper, more resourced, better understood, and of a higher quality.

Yet the perennial issue of time comes back around to haunt us. This attempt, feedback and revise cycle requires time. Teachers need time to plan how to utilise these metacognitive strategies. They need time to review their effectiveness, hold professional conversations, seek out feedback, and make changes to their progress. They need time to amend the curriculum, share best practice and support the embedding and deepening of metacognition within their subject curriculum. Yet this should not be too great an issue if we are aware that it may be a potential barrier in the first instance.

Firstly, changes should be limited, both for teachers' sake, but also to ensure we remain true to metacognitive theory and implement it most effectively. Secondly, you will hopefully already have time carved out for curriculum development, whether during whole school PD opportunities or faculty specific time. Hence, these blocks of time provide opportunities to reflect on the latest curriculum development area – metacognition. Thirdly, systems should be in place to support with consistent curriculum development outside of these times. Curriculum development needs to be active, rather than static, after all.

'The power of the abstract is prone to mutate'

This quote, by Ruth Ashbee, in their book *Curriculum: Theory, Culture and the Subject Specialisms* (2021), is extraordinarily apt for the implementation of metacognition, itself perhaps the most abstract of all teaching and learning approaches that we may attempt to implement.

Ashbee goes on to warn that where the abstract is prone to (lethal) mutations, it may move into the 'folly of the generic' (p. 31). In essence, where approaches are not clearly structured, informed by subject specific approach, re-affirmed with high-quality training, and complemented with examples and resources, they risk becoming generic in their implementation.

This is arguably what has happened with metacognition more generally over recent years, where schools have attempted to make changes to aid a metacognitive approach within their walls. Where a clear understanding of the theory is lacking, or (and) changes are not conscious of disciplinary individualism, or (and) changes are not fleshed out with examples or resources, implementation will likely become generic. That is, implementation will not be sensitive to the subtleties of subject disciplines, nor will approaches be chosen at times where they are most suited, but instead included to meet an overall aim of 'include metacognition'.

We therefore have several points that we need to consider to ensure that our implementation does not become generic, or worse, lethally mutated (where implementation is so far removed from the theory that not only are positive impacts not found, but negative impacts actually occur).

The first is that changes must be deeply embedded within the curriculum. Not a whole school teaching and learning policy, but within the confines of a subject discipline. Approaches need to be specific, and sensitive, to an individual subject area (which once again, provides the rationale for the latter half of this book). Consistent training of staff is also imperative, and will be covered later in this chapter. Thirdly, the continuous engagement with these changes, to adapt and mould them to the curriculum, ensuring their appropriateness, rather than their generalism, is also crucial, building on the earlier point around sustaining changes through revision of curricula changes. Finally, exemplar and resource development is crucial, and should be a major part of annual progress checks. Imagine joining a department four years into their metacognitive journey, seeing exactly where metacognition fits in their curriculum, but having no examples of how to do this, or resources to support implementation in your own classroom. In this scenario, the member of staff would struggle to remain aligned to the metacognitive implementation seem in other classrooms, just due to the lack of scaffolding that they have to support with their implementation of the curriculum.

Creator versus implementor

One concept from Ashbee now gives way to another, this time considering the implications of a creator versus an implementor. In their book on curriculum (2021), Ashbee rightly argues that where the curriculum is developed by one person, but merely provided to others without opportunity for discussion, its power will not be as great for others as it would be in the hands of the designer. In effect, Ashbee is getting at the point that a creator – be that of curriculum, resources, a lesson or so forth – will understand the *what* and *why* behind the document. Only they will understand the purpose of the document, how it links together and how it supports other teaching in its full depth.

We can imagine this situation with ease. Consider situations where you have been provided with a lesson, or lessons, to deliver to students, regardless of whether that has been in your own curriculum area, or another. These lessons were designed by an individual, with their own approach and methods in mind. When we receive these resources, they never *quite* suit our own approach, or the way that we model or deliver content. Individualisation is required. For the creator, they are perfect lessons that are extremely powerful, though.

In this scenario, where a curriculum document is made and amended by only one, or a small group of individuals, they will understand the true purpose and power of these changes. But where time is not invested into ensuring that others who will be utilising this document understand this too, the power that it holds is reduced. In short, if others are not involved with the implementation, or latterly, the revisions of the curriculum, they will not truly understand it, or the connections, without significant opportunity for training and professional conversation. Thus, we either need to ensure all current (and future staff) have the opportunity to engage with the updating and future revision of the metacognitive changes of the curriculum, or that sufficient time needs to be given on a consistent basis to allow for these conversations and training. Without it, changes will not be sustained or as powerful (or consistent), as they could be.

Training

Unsurprisingly, training will play a key part of sustaining and embedding any and all metacognitive changes that you make to your curriculum. Again, it has been clear throughout the importance of training for several different reasons, including:

- Developing a deep understanding of metacognitive theory, and the importance of this in relation to effective implementation.
- To support with ensuring the power of the resources in the hands of the creator is also vested in those who will be aiding with the implementation.
- To ensure that implementation is specific and concrete, as opposed to abstract and risking generalisation.

Yet, there is more to training than just these reasons. These provide us with the cruciality of initial training, but do not say much as to future training requirements to support embedding and sustaining of changes. Unfortunately, what future training requirements are, will be specific to the progress that is made with initial implementation, changes in staffing, and end of year progress markers, among other aims. Therefore, to determine training requirements to ensure embedding and sustaining of changes will need to consider some of the following:

- Ensuring that new members of staff are trained in general metacognitive theory, as well as how metacognition is embedded within their curriculum areas and developing knowledge of the strategies that students are accustomed with.
- Ensuring that training is subject specific, to ensure that metacognitive development is sensitive to the demands of the subject discipline, rather than being generic.
- Ensuring that training supports all departments to reach year-end goals across the course of several years of implementation and embedding of metacognition into the curriculum.
- Ensuring that training is responsive to QA, student feedback, teacher feedback, and other data points as part of wider triangulation.

Though this may appear vague, for implementation, and latterly, embedding and sustaining of changes to be successful, it is a unique, context specific plan that is required around training. One approach will not fit all, and so your own determinations, against the factors signposted above, and other considerations that you deem fit, will need to be made. It should also be noted that if other key points around curriculum development have been heeded, for example those around generalised curricula, or mutations of implementation, then points of embedding and sustaining metacognitive developments are similar to how you would look to embed and sustain any other, long term pedagogical change in a school.

Codified documents

Throughout this chapter, comment has been made on taking a long-term approach to implementation, considering active ingredients and effective short-term, and longer-term, training. Where curricula changes have been made, they need to continue to be evaluated and refined, both within the curriculum and in teaching. Crucially, as time develops, examples of when and how metacognitive strategies are used within the curriculum should be available with examples and resources, for where metacognition lives in the curriculum as an abstract context, its true power will never be released. Many examples are given in the subject specific chapters that follow, which will provide you with a starting point as to which strategies can be utilised, and where, within your curriculum. As understanding grows, and strategies used more extensively, exactly where they are utilised effectively ought to be codified.

Quite how these examples and resources should appear matters less, and again will be subject and context specific. Yet, Ashbee again raises key points on this area. Discussing the curriculum more generally, they wrote that a codified curriculum will include such documents as a booklet of reading, resources, model answers and practice questions. These resources, Ashbee discusses in their book on curriculum, should be carefully chosen, with written explanations, clear models and practice, consistent available. This curriculum should then consistently be implemented by all teachers with all classes and all students. Where a curriculum is this well-resourced, not interpreting and implementing it effectively or in-line with overall aims is a challenge in and of itself!

We must consider therefore, that if good curriculum planning takes in all of these documents, that therefore good metacognitive curriculum must also take in all of these factors. Through the codification of the metacognitive strategies that we choose to specifically complement our curriculum, we aid the possibility of effective implementation, improve the likelihood of useful professional conversations, and of supporting new staff when they join a department area.

What might this look like, then?

- Clear signposting within the curriculum as to where different metacognitive strategies can be utilised.
- A bank of strategy resources to complement the curriculum.
- Explanation within a unit plan as to how the metacognitive strategy can be utilised effectively.
- Presentation notes, where strategies are in-built to pre-prepared lessons.
- A metacognitive faculty guidebook, outlining what the strategies look like in that subject discipline.

Once again, what this looks like for a given subject area will vary by the documents that they already possess, how planning and collaboration occurs, and the format of their curriculum, but the above does provide a set of ways in which metacognitive implementation can be codified.

References

Ashbee, R. (2021). *Curriculum: Theory, Culture and the Subject Specialisms*. London: Routledge.

Howard, K., & Hill, C. (2020). *Symbiosis: The Curriculum and the Classroom*. Melton: John Catt Educational.

Myatt, M. (2018). *The Curriculum: Gallimaufry to Coherence*. Melton: John Catt Educational.

Sharples, J., Albers, B., Fraser, S., & Kime, S. (2018). *Putting Evidence to Work: A School's Guide to Implementation*. London: Education Endowment Foundation.

5

Whole schools versus subject-specific implementation

Nathan Burns

But we're already doing it!

One of the most common pushbacks that I find, and you will too, in all likelihood, is staff saying that they are already being metacognitive in their classrooms; the strategies that you are introducing are nothing new, and this is just more work and policy for the sake of it. We need to acknowledge that there is a lot of strength to this argument. The strategies that I have provided in my previous books, as well as this one, are not necessarily ground-breaking. The wheel has not been re-invented. I have not somehow managed to design strategies to make all students strategic metacognitive practitioners overnight. What we instead have are a range of different approaches, to modelling, questioning, evaluation, and so forth, that can all be utilised in order to develop students' metacognitive abilities. It must be remembered that it is how we utilise resources in the classroom that determines the benefits that they bring and the skills that students will subsequently develop. Therefore, staff may already be utilising some of the strategies discussed in the second half of this book. However, the big change is paying attention to the metacognitive aspects of all of these strategies, as it is possible to use many of these strategies without even a cursory glance at the metacognitive benefits that they can bring.

Therefore, what angle do we use? We need to acknowledge that many of these strategies are not new, and teachers will already be using some of them. We also need to acknowledge that teachers will already be, to an extent, developing metacognitive skills of students through the approaches and language that they are using in their classroom. The aim of developing our metacognitive approach is:

a To shine more light on the invisibility of metacognition in order to improve (and sustain) improvements in students' metacognitive abilities.

b   To ensure that metacognitive development becomes a priority for our teaching, as opposed to a consequential benefit that comes from our current teaching approaches.

c   To ensure consistently of high-quality practice both within, and across faculty areas.

d   To ensure that a common whole-school approach can be taken to further strengthen metacognitive teaching and progress of students.

e   To ensure that staff have the very best strategies at their fingertips to develop metacognition and know *when* they are best utilised.

f   To ensure that staff are supported, through the delivery of the very best PD on metacognition.

g   To sustain metacognitive developments through the codification of approaches into curriculum documents.

h   To ensure that positive metacognitive gains can be sustained over the long-term.

i   To complement other whole-school and/or faculty work around others areas of foci such as modelling, questioning or feedback.

j   To ensure that students are consistently getting the highest quality teaching that they possibly can be.

When leading school implementation, we need to level with staff. Enforcing change where staff believe that they are already doing a required activity, or using necessary language, is not going to go down well! Instead, we must acknowledge what is already being done (which is also crucial when developing a 5-year plan and annual progress targets anyhow), and build from there, supporting staff and sharing the bigger picture.

The priority – subject specificity

In determining that metacognition is so incredibly powerful, as we did in chapter 1, we begin to consider the importance of consistent approaches across the whole school. If metacognition is as important as the research says that it can be, then surely we need consistent and high-quality approaches across the whole school? While consistency across a whole school, embedded with a whole school approach and training *can* be helpful, we must be cautious. Ashbee (2021) wrote of the fear of brute force implementation. In this scenario, top-down approaches can be 'devastating to the integrity of the subjects and the fidelity of curriculum thinking' (p. 31). We wouldn't (or at least, shouldn't!) enforce top-down curriculum changes which are not sensitive to the individuality of a given curriculum area. Instead, we need to be guided by subject expertise in order to determine the curriculum that they need to teach, the sequencing of it, and the best subject-specific pedagogical approaches to complement this. Yes, we will have whole school approaches that are common to all areas, such as retrieval practice, plenary tasks, assessment, and behavioural expectations, perhaps, but again these must be run through the subject-lens, to ensure that they are done in an appropriate manner for the subject area. Consider a 'last lesson, last week, last month, last term' retrieval starter, which works beautifully in a Maths lesson, but hopelessly in a practical PE lesson. The best ways to go about these changes is through considering the subject-specific lens.

The same is so very true of the metacognitive approaches that we must take. As has been determined, the meta-aspects relate to the cognitive actions. Where cognition changes, as it does within a subject domain, let alone between subjects, the meta-cognitive evaluations made, and strategies required, will also fluctuate. If they did not, the latter half of this book, exploring what metacognitive strategies look like in different subject areas, would not be required! Therefore, what metacognitive planning looks like in one subject, will be completely different from how it looks in a different subject area. Once again, consider the broad nature of disciplinary knowledge taught across school, ranging from drama to maths, PE to MFL. Though there are swathes of similarities, there are significantly more differences. A one-approach fits all metacognitive strategy will not work. The approaches required to facilitate metacognitive development need to be determined at a subject level, and not a whole-school level, however much this rubs against the desire for a common whole-school approach and level of consistency.

Trust in subject expertise

Where we have a strong subject expert as a department leader, we need to trust in them and their subject expertise. It is these members of staff who we need to drive forward the embedding and sustaining of metacognition within their curriculum. It is these members of staff who will be delivering feedback to colleagues, making amendments to subject-specific approaches, and ensuring that subject-specific metacognitive professional development is offered.

This is not, however, to say that these members of staff will not need support. It would be unwise, to say the least, to tell subject leaders that they need to embed metacognitive strategies within their curriculum with no guidance, further support, or training themselves. A balance must instead be struck! Furthermore, the subject expertise of the leader must be considered. In conversations during the process of writing this book with Ruth Ashbee, this exact point was discussed. It is subject expertise which must guide the metacognitive changes that subsequently are implemented – whether this expertise come from a subject leader, as they often will, a senior leader, or even an external advisor.

Further to this point, there are some avenues that senior leaders can support with:

1 Providing whole-school training on metacognition, so that staff are aware of why it is so important (and level with staff, as highlighted in the first section of this chapter), and what the theory actually says.
2 Scoping out time for faculties to consider which metacognitive strategies work for them, and then how and when they will embed them within the classroom.
3 Providing long-term sustained opportunity for curriculum revision.
4 Supporting faculty leaders with QA of metacognitive developments both in codified documents, as well as through learning walks.
5 Supporting faculty leaders in providing subject-specific PD for their teams.

Beyond these areas, it is best that we are instead trusting of our subject leaders to design a metacognitive approach for their curriculum area. Implementation is likelier to be truer to the theory, more specific to the curriculum, and allow for more staff to be creators of these approaches and resources, as opposed to just deliverers. Therefore, senior leaders must support with whole-school support where it is suitable, but in the main, provide the time, space and expertise for subject leaders and teachers to develop their own subject-specific metacognitive approaches.

Where a whole-school approach *can* work

But all of this is not to say that a whole-school approach is not warranted, or indeed, suitable, at certain times on the implementation journey. Caveats to this approach have been illuminated within the start of this chapter, for good reason. Let us consider the following example from Kat Howard and Claire Hill, in their 2020 book, *Symbiosis; the Curriculum and the Classroom*. In the book, they wrote that there can be no overarching curricula model for all disciplines. In practice, this means that cross-subject generic templates and excessive scripting can stifle the curriculum, teacher and students, and also pose a high risk of misinterpretation. Through developing a whole school approach to metacognitive developing, through such documents as scripting or generic templates, would likely see the end result as detailed by Howard and Hill.

Yet, a level of commonality can be developed. Primarily, this will be through whole school training of staff, ensuring that all are up-to-speed with exactly why metacognition is imperative, and what it *actually* is (easier said than done)! But this can also be done through the type of strategies that are provided for faculty areas to consider.

In the latter half of this book, subject experts provide you with in-depth examples and narrative around how a range of metacognition strategies can be successfully used within those curriculum areas. However, the strategies that these experts used are grouped into three areas: planning, monitoring and evaluation. Moreover, the strategies that these experts drew from were ones that I provided to them. I didn't enforce *which* strategies they must use, but rather requested that they detail three appropriate strategies for their subject area in each of the three categories – planning, monitoring, and evaluation. What you will notice is a huge amount of commonality in the approaches that these subjects' experts chose! The same strategies can often be used successfully across a range of different subject disciplines. In the same way that retrieval practice can be used in every subject area, it just looks subtly different for each context, the same is true of these approaches. So, what does this mean?

Primarily, it means that we should work backwards, allowing subject areas to choose strategies that work for their subject areas, with common-sense dictating that the latter half of this book will do much of the work for them. Once determined, faculties can feedback on the approaches that they are wanting to use, and in all likelihood, you will also find that there is significant cross-over in the strategies that are being used.

This then allows us to produce a policy, codified document, or whatever we may want to call it that talks of the metacognitive strategies that you would see around the school. Where there is no commonality of strategy across most or all subject areas, there is one guaranteed cross-over – that of having strategies that support students' abilities to plan, monitor and evaluate (or an alternative area, should you wish to change the meta-cognitive focus, as driven by discussions in Chapter 3).

This approach to whole-school policymaking will allow us to ensure the subject specificity, and sensitivity, is at the forefront of our consideration and implementation, but will also then allow us to move on to design a whole-school approach. This surely, is the best of both worlds.

It may be however, that you decide that you do not want to do focus on planning, monitoring, and evaluation, but rather the area of modelling or questioning perhaps, or maybe even a wicked problem like developing independent problems. Once again, we can ensure consistency across school, through identifying the type of strategies that are going to be developed across all subject disciplines (e.g., modelling strategies, process strategies, discussion strategies, and so forth), and also providing a limited number of approaches, as I did, with my subject experts. This again would allow us to consider the subject specificity in the first instance, but also ensure a commonality and consistency of approach across school.

There are benefits to subject areas, and students, of having this level of consistency. Consider a situation where each faculty area was focussing on a different area of met-acognitive development, and hence a different set of metacognitive strategies. The number of new metacognitive ideas that we would be expecting students to consider would be vast. The amount of practice of each strategy would be diminished, with each strategy seeming specific to that one subject area, thus meaning that metacognitive development of students was slowed. Moreover, where students see approaches in only one subject area, they may believe that those approaches *only* work in that subject area, rather than considering how they can use that approach in other areas, too. Thus, through a narrowing of the approaches utilised at any given point, we find that met-acognitive development in one area can complement and develop the metacognitive development in another.

Whole-school consistency can also be found in other ways, and not just by limiting the area, or range of strategies, that faculty areas can choose from (or adapt, where necessary). How implementation occurs can, or rather should, be done in a consistent manner. As outlined in Chapter 3, it is the depth of strategy use, rather than the range of strategies used, that is best. Subject areas would not be doing better by utilising more strategies in their curriculum, but rather, through using the handful of strategies they choose more consistently, more frequently, and ensuring that they were embedded within the curriculum, and resourced and exemplified. Once again, this can allow a consistency, through outlining how many strategies a subject area should be focussing on at any one point, and support can be given to ensure the embedding of the strategy. Moreover, we know that effective implementation will occur through a deep embedding and use of a strategy, rather than a surface-level approach to a vast number of different strategies.

Overall, we need to appreciate that subject individualism must come first. So long as this is the first layer of implementation, we can, at a zoomed-out level, tie together approaches that multiple faculty areas are using, provide common training to all staff, and direct a common and effective way for the implementing, embedding, and sustaining of these changes. Through this approach, a strong balance will be kept between subject specific agency and whole-school consistency and structure.

Developing a common language

Howard and Hill (2020) wrote that subject experts are the ones best placed to determine the common language required in their subject area to use explicitly with students. Though this may be true of the subject discipline curriculum, it is perhaps only partially true for metacognition.

Regardless of the need for a subject specific approach for metacognitive strategy choice, initial moves towards developing metacognition in a school should start from whole-school training. A consistent understanding of the *why* and *what* behind metacognition is imperative to implementation. This means, therefore, that a common language ought to be developed from this point forward. One teachers' definition of metacognition ought to be the same as another's; one teacher's use of the phrase 'knowledge of self' need be the same as any other teacher; one teachers' description of a tacit metacognitive individual should be same as that from any other member of staff (and so forth).

Through ensuring consistent whole-staff training, this should not be a problem. Where this language is commonly understood, professional conversations will be aided, the ability to critique and think critically in this area of metacognition improved, and implementation will be more consistent. Risk of (lethal) mutation will thus be lower.

Regardless of the approaches taken within a subject area, the language of metacognition will not really vary. What planning may look like in say, history, versus maths, will be different, but that planning is broken down into a consideration of knowledge of task, self and strategies, would not be.

It would be therefore pertinent to consider the common language that you want to hear in your school. The following words or phrases should, I argue, be commonly understood by all members of staff (though you may determine further words and phrases need to be included within this list).

- Metacognition
- Planning
- Monitoring
- Evaluation
- Knowledge of task
- Knowledge of self

- Knowledge of strategies
- Tacit (learner)
- Aware (learner)
- Strategic (learner)
- Reflective (learner)
- Cognition
- Self-regulation

If training is successful, then all staff will not only be able to define these words and phrases, but build them into conversations effectively. Much like a student doesn't know a topic until they can apply the disciplinary knowledge, do teachers *really* understand metacognition until these phrases are used commonly and correctly in professional conversation and curriculum development work?

Forget the data

A point that has weaved in and out of this book so far is around data. Measuring metacognition is an extremely hard task, and monitoring metacognitive progress in even a vague manner, such as using the levels determined by Perkins (1992), comes with its own set of difficulties. This means, therefore, that we cannot easily measure the impact our new approaches are having on the metacognitive abilities of students. A range of ways to monitor progress have been given, especially in Chapter 5, but in conclusion to these chapters on the curriculum more generally, I wanted to leave you with one final thought, based upon work from a number of authors, but including Sealy (2020), Howard and Hill (2020), Ashbee (2021), and Myatt (2018) – titans of UK curriculum work. Read these books, or any of their work and one thing is clear. Curriculum development should be measured not through grades, but through the process by which it is improving: the subject specific training; curriculum evaluation; curriculum improvement; resource development; self-reflection; professional conversations, and so many other (non-grade) factors. Where this is true for curriculum development, the same is true for developing metacognitive curriculum development. We know that a stronger curriculum will, in time, lead to improved outcomes. But we don't, or shouldn't, attempt to measure the strength of a curriculum by the grades that students get each year. The same is true with metacognitive development. Trust the process. Make sure it is strong. Make sure it is robust. Keep it as a focus. Keep working at it. The gains will come.

References

Ashbee, R. (2021). *Curriculum: Theory, Culture and the Subject Specialisms*. London: Routledge.

Howard, K., and Hill, C. (2020). *Symbiosis: The Curriculum and the Classroom*. Melton: John
    Catt Educational.
Myatt, M. (2018). *The Curriculum: Gallimaufry to Coherence*. Melton: John Catt Educational.
Perkins, D. N. (1992). *Smart Schools: Better Thinking and Learning for Every Child*. New York:
    Free Press.
Sealy, C. (Ed.) (2020). *The ResearchED Guide to The Curriculum: An Evidence-Informed Guide
    for Teachers*. Woodbridge: John Catt Educational.

6

Strategy choices

Nathan Burns

Introduction

The curriculum theorising is done. Subject-specific implementation versus whole school structure has been debated. What success looks like has been determined. Now, it is time for the strategies!

Across the next few chapters, covering all major subject areas, and written by some of the best thinkers in these subject areas, a range of high-quality metacognitive strategies will be covered. Each author has been tasked with choosing three strategies for the areas of planning, monitoring and evaluation (the three parts of regulation of cognition).

To ensure some level of consistency, and to avoid this book becoming many pages longer than it already is, each author chose strategies from the list below. Each of the strategies is defined and explained within this chapter, allowing chapters authors to focus on *when* and *how* to use these strategies, rather than describing the fundamental of what each strategy actually is.

Following on from this chapter, you will find highly detailed, subject-specific chapters, providing you with the information that you need about what exactly metacognition looks like in your subject area! But first, the strategies.

Planning

Let us first consider strategies relating to planning.

Graphic organisers

Graphic organisers are visual tools, with each type focussing on a different type of thinking (see Table 6.1).

Table 6.1 Types of graphic organiser

Name	Type of thinking
Circle map	Defining within a context
Bubble map	(Concise) description
Double bubble map	Compare and contrast

(Continued)

Table 6.1 Types of graphic organiser *(Continued)*

Name	Type of thinking
Flow map	Sequence (of events)
Multi-flow map	Cause and effect
Fishbone	Causation
Tree map	Classification (related)
Brace maps	Constituent parts of one thing
Bridge map	Analogies
Frayer model	Research into one idea

Where an appropriate organiser is chosen, it can help students plan out an effective response to a task, concentrating their thinking on the type of approach required to successfully complete a task.

Planning documents

The planning document draws upon the metacognitive cycle of: knowledge of task, knowledge of self and knowledge of task. Students would complete this grid, shown in Table 6.2, as their planning, before completing a specific task. This grid ensures that students have considered the three fundamental parts of planning.

Table 6.2 An example planning document grid

Knowledge of task	Knowledge of self	Knowledge of strategies
What must I do to complete this task?	What relevant curriculum knowledge do I have for this task?	What are the different strategies that I can use to complete this task?
What time do I have?	What knowledge will I need to get, and how?	How do they vary in their utility?
What must I include within my answer?		What are their relative strengths and weaknesses?
What is my comprehension of this task?		

Problem-solving grids

This planning document is similar to the previous strategy. In this grid, students complete the first three boxes of 'comprehension', 'connections', and 'strategies', before then completing the task, and later filling in the 'evaluation' box.

It is possible to place the task in the centre of this document, similarly to a *Frayer Model*.

This strategy helps to ensure that students take time to consider their approach to a task, as well as utilising evaluation from similarly completed tasks previously (Table 6.3).

Table 6.3 An example problem-solving grid

Comprehension	Connection
What is the task asking you to do?	When have you encountered a similar problem?
What are the key works in the task?	What is the same and what is different?
What relevant information have you been provided with and how may this help?	How will your evaluation from the connected task help you in this task?
Strategies	**Evaluation**
What are the different strategies that I can use to complete this task?	What went well, and how do you know?
	Was your strategy choice effective?
How do they vary in their utility?	Have you met the task criteria?
What are their relative strengths and weaknesses?	What would you do differently next time?

Exam question analysis

This strategy proposes that you present students with a range of high-quality (exam) question answers. These answers are then analysed – this can be teacher-led, pair, or group work, or individually – in order to identify the factors that make the answer of such a high quality.

Students then utilise these identified factors to help plan out their response to a similar exam question to the one just analysed.

Use of this strategy ensures that students are attempting to incorporate high-quality aspects into their answers.

Key word quizzing

Key word quizzing is a strategy utilised to develop a student's core understanding of question terminology. For example, do students know what *discuss* or *evaluate* mean? This strategy is often utilised through teacher-led modelling, where expert thinking illuminates the meanings of these key words. Follow-up question can then be used to ensure that students are confident and clear on these key words. Improvements in the area of key words helps improve students' independent comprehension of tasks that they are given and will strengthen their planning abilities.

Strategy evaluation

A teacher-led strategy, here, the different approaches that can be taken to complete a task are explored. This could be through modelling, or questioning, and discussion. The range of strategies appropriate to complete a task would be discussed, as well as the relative strengths, weaknesses and utilities of each approach. The purpose of this strategy is to ensure that students think through the approaches that they can take, to increase the efficiency and effectiveness of their work.

Knowledge organisers

Knowledge organisers (or drivers, documents, or whatever they are called in your school) collate the core content information that students need to know in a given topic area. Knowledge organisers can be used to support students in planning for a task through supplementing their knowledge on a certain topic area. They also ensure that knowledge organisers are not just static documents, but something that is incorporated within the learning of students.

Limited questions

This strategy suggests providing a limit to the number of questions that each (or all) students can ask. Rather than limiting the support that students can get, the aim of this strategy is to ensure that students are asking questions which are both specific and precisely isolate the information that they *really* do need. This helps students to prioritise the support and information that they need in order to complete a specific task.

Monitoring

The following strategies are concerned with monitoring.

Checklists

Here, either the class teacher or students will produce a list of all of the steps that they need to go through to complete a task – almost like a little list. Ideally, it will also be chronological, too. This list provides a 'tick list' to ensure that students complete all of the stages that they need to work through for successful task completion.

Key questions

When presented with a more significant task or problem, this strategy suggests that it should be broken down into mini sub-questions. When students then begin to respond to the task, they are able to work through each of these key, or sub, questions in turn. Through doing this, we increase the likelihood that students respond to all parts of the task as required. This also helps to reduce cognitive load, as students are freed up to concentrate completely on content.

Content checklists

This strategy focuses on the 'knowledge of self' part of metacognition. Here, students will record down all of the relevant information that they know *ought* to be included within a successful response to a task. While completing the task, students can cross off each piece of information once they have included it. This helps ensure that all key information is included in a task response and increases the likelihood it is included at a suitable point in the response.

Strategy success criteria

Once students have identified, in the planning stage, the most suitable strategy to use to approach a given task, this strategy suggests that the key stages in that strategy can then be recorded. This then provides students with a further checklist from which they can work through, reducing the likelihood that they utilise the strategy incorrectly (for example, missing out steps or mis-ordering steps). It also reduces the load students face from recalling relevant information and strategy stages, and instead frees thinking up to focus predominantly on just the former area.

Task success criteria

This monitoring strategy focuses on the comprehension of a given task. The teacher or student(s) will produce a list, based on the task criteria or marking rubric, of all of the factors that are required in a task response or answer. This ensures that students are working through these in their answer to a given question and do not miss out any key criteria in their response to a question.

Warning signs

This content-specific strategy looks to identify key misconceptions that may arise for a given task (warning signs or 'red flags'). This provides a guide to students as to what they should *not* have in their task response. It helps to ensure that changes to a response can be made sooner (i.e. 'oh no, that shouldn't have happened, let me go back a stage now') rather than at the end of a task where students may have run out of time (or motivation) to restart or review their answer.

Flow maps

The majority of the monitoring strategies above can be placed within the visual 'flow map'. The flow map places information in a chronological order, but importantly, translates written information into something visual. This flow map can be especially useful for strategies such as the checklist strategy or the strategy success criteria strategy. Once again, this provides students with a clear structure to move through and reduces the cognitive load of recalling content and comprehending the task in the same instance.

Evaluation

The next set of strategies concern evaluation.

Wrappers

Wrappers are used following an assessment (typically end-of-term, so it is larger) or a mock exam. Wrappers can be adapted to suit the subject or assessment, but typically record, in a table, each of the questions, as well as reasons for dropped marks, such as 'not reading the question' or 'misunderstood the question requirements'. Students then identify the common reasons for the dropping of marks.

Typically, a wrapper will include directed questions on its reverse, such as 'how long did you revise for?' and 'what was your revision environment like?'

This strategy forces students to consider where they dropped marks, supports them in identifying trends in their weaknesses and forces consideration as to the preparation (or lack there-of) for the assessment.

Self/peer marking

In a re-working of a common strategy, students will self or peer mark, but they will also look to identify areas of strength and areas of improvement, rather than just providing an overall mark or grade. Through doing this, students are having to think deeper about the relative strengths and weaknesses of a response, the task criteria and effective next steps to improve themselves or their colleagues' work.

Plenary tasks

Plenary tasks can take one of two forms – a content assessment or a metacognitive assessment. A content assessment might provide students with a handful of questions on the topic(s) covered during that teaching period and allow students to evaluate what it is they have understood and their next steps to improve. A metacognitive assessment may include questions around when a certain strategy may be used or identifying (self) areas for improvement.

These tasks can be utilised by the teacher to inform future planning or held by the students to support their own learning journey and place onus on them to direct their improvements.

Reflection tasks

The strategy proposes that students end a period of learning through having a directed reflection task. This could include students identifying areas that require improvement, consideration of common mistakes that they are making and identifying areas that they may need support within. By blocking out a set of time to do this, it ensures that students are actively reflecting, rather than it being a passive activity crammed in to the final 30 seconds of a lesson.

Answering directed questions

This strategy places emphasis on students evaluating one pre-determined area of their thinking, such as planning, monitoring, or evaluation. In order to evaluate this area, students would be provided with clear (directed) questions through which they need to work. For example, if students were being asked to evaluate how successful their planning technique was for a given task, they may be asked questions such as:

- What planning technique did you use and why?
- What were the strengths and weaknesses of your planning technique?

- Did you include sufficient, insufficient, or too much depth to your planning?
- Would you go about planning for this task in a different way next time?

Through asking tight, and pre-determined questions, this strategy ensures that students have to drill down on evaluation in one particular area.

Informing future planning

This strategy proposes that as soon as students have finished evaluating one task, that they *immediately* utilise this evaluation to inform the planning for a similar task (and then repeat the process). The rationale for this is that often, evaluation can become static – a student can self-evaluate, or be provided with feedback, but if it is not utilised (i.e. it is static), it becomes wasted. Through ensuring that students *instantly* utilise this feedback (or self-evaluation) in planning, it ensures that it becomes actioned and begins to improve a student's abilities forthwith.

New strategy

The importance of alternative strategies for approaching a task cannot be under-estimated. If students are more confident with a range of strategies, and their relative utilities, strengths and weaknesses, they will become more efficient and effective learners – able to adapt to a wider range of tasks. One way in which to improve this is to get students to repeat a task, but utilising an alternative strategy. Students are then able to directly compare two (or more) approaches to a task and continue to establish the strengths, weaknesses and utilities of different approaches.

Good, better, and best answers

A tweaking of the popular strategy 'good, better, best' answer, this strategy proposes that students are supported (by the teacher or in groups), in their evaluation of three different responses to a question. These responses should be extremely similar in their grading (for example, a high six ranging through to a high seven or low eight), so that there are only subtle differences in the quality of the exam responses. Why different answers are graded higher than each other can then be established, illuminating to students the small factors that they must include within their answers in order to improve their own grades. Additionally, where suitable responses are chosen, it may be that an answer which has a lower grade has some features that are better than the other two responses presented. Once again, this makes for a depth of evaluation and helps develop students understanding as to the factors that make different parts of, and a full answer, higher quality.

Learning diaries

A learning diary provides students with the opportunity to keep a record of their learning, particularly their identified areas of strength and the areas that they need to improve and revise. This diary could be completed with other tasks identified above, such as directed questions or plenary tasks. Through keeping an accurate log of learning progress, there are hopefully two main benefits. The first is (self) motivation, where students can see the progress that they have made across topics, strategies and meta-cognitive factors. The second is that the diary provides a personalised revision list when assessments come up in the curriculum.

PMI grids

The PMI grid – or Plus, Minus, Interesting grid – is a soft-touch way for students to consider their learning during a lesson. This grid allows students to consider something that they have done successfully, an area that they need to improve and something which piqued their interest. For example, this document could then be used to inform future teacher planning, provide curriculum feedback or be used within a learning diary.

Conclusion

And there we have it – a range of highly effective strategies to support the development of students planning, monitoring, and evaluation skills. Over the coming chapters, subject experts will detail which of these strategies are suitable for their subject areas and exactly how they use them, providing examples as they go. So, let us begin with mathematics.

Part II
Curriculum areas

Part II
Curriculum areas

7

Mathematics

Ryan Woolaston

Introduction

Mathematics is all about solving problems, problems that require logical reasoning and abstract thinking, and metacognition plays a pivotal role in this process. It helps students realise their potential and become effective problem solvers. As mathematics teachers, we often question how best to teach problem-solving and whether it can even be explicitly taught at all. According to Geary (2012), problem-solving is a biologically primary skill, an instinctive ability we evolved as a necessary adaptation for survival and resource management. We acquire biologically primary skills through experience and observation rather than direct instruction. For example, when you learnt to walk, you may have watched others and received a helping hand from a parent, but the core mechanics of balance, cadence, and pressure were instinctively learnt but not taught. The ability to learn these skills and acquire certain knowledge is hardwired into us through evolutionary necessity. The same is true of problem-solving; our ancestors were not formally taught how to solve problems, yet (thankfully for us) they figured it out.

In contrast, mathematics is considered biologically secondary knowledge, which requires explicit teaching and learning. Unlike biologically primary skills, biologically secondary knowledge like mathematics is not instinctive and must be formally taught. While general problem-solving skills may come naturally, applying them to complex areas like Mathematics demands a solid foundation of domain-specific knowledge. Therefore, it is essential that we explicitly teach this secondary knowledge and ensure students gain depth and fluency before they can effectively apply their innate problem-solving abilities to the mathematical domain.

Geary's distinction helps highlight why problem-solving in mathematics requires more than instinct, it demands conscious reflection and strategy development, which metacognitive skills can foster. This tension between instinctive problem-solving and the need for explicit teaching explains why planning and implementing effective problem-solving lessons in mathematics can be so challenging (Kramarski, 2008). A potential solution lies in the careful integration of metacognitive strategies. Metacognition provides students with the tools to navigate and connect these two types of knowledge, accelerating their development as problem solvers within the realm of mathematics.

The action of problem-solving is defined by Pate and Miller (2011) as efforts towards achieving a situational goal for which there is no direct solution. This means that students will need to process, interpret, hypothesise, analyse solution strategies and have the resilience to deal with solutions which are not successful. All of these are skills that can be enhanced by expanding a student's metacognitive toolkit.

Susanto et al. (2023) make the argument that developing strong metacognitive thinking skills is a crucial element for mathematical learning and problem-solving. These skills allow students to reflect on their strategies, consider alternatives, and make necessary adjustments. There exists a significant correlation between metacognitive skills and problem-solving success, suggesting strongly that more detailed instruction in metacognitive strategies can lead to greatly improved problem-solving performance (Temel, 2013).

So what does all this mean for me when I am teaching bottom set Year 9 on a cold Friday afternoon. The key takeaway is that once students have a solid foundation of domain-specific knowledge, we can enhance their ability to problem-solve by utilising metacognitive strategies. Like any strategy or skill, this should not be a one-off; it needs to be a steady, regular diet of metacognition built into the fabric of your planning. In the following pages, I will share metacognitive strategies that you can implement in your maths lessons – yes, even with Year 9, on a cold Friday afternoon!

Planning

Let us first consider strategies relating to planning.

Key word quizzing

In early mathematics education, the connection between vocabulary, both in size and complexity and mathematical ability, is particularly pronounced. Slusser et al. indicate that a strong foundation in number word knowledge correlates with improved mathematical proficiency as students transition into more formal mathematical education (Slusser et al., 2018). This underscores the vital importance of explicit vocabulary instruction in the maths classroom, as it not only supports comprehension but also develops confidence and alleviates any early onset maths anxiety (Bringula et al., 2021).

Mathematics has its own highly specialised language, yet many of its terms have different meanings in everyday contexts. Consider these examples:

- Product – Is it the result of multiplication or something manufactured?
- Pi(e) – A transcendental number or a delicious dessert?
- Translation – A geometric transformation or converting between languages?

Beyond these, mathematical vocabulary is often misused, both in the real world and even in classrooms. One common frustration is hearing a series of calculations referred to as 'sums' when in fact sum only applies to addition. Similarly, it is easy to confuse negative (a state) with minus (an operation) – something I have been guilty of myself frequently.

Let us also consider the growing number of students in our classrooms who do not have English as a first language. Having worked internationally for the past seven years and prior to this in wonderfully diverse inner-city schools in Nottingham and Coventry, I am acutely aware of the importance of mathematical language and keywords. A study on English Medium Instruction in Taiwan (Huang & Chou, 2024) showed that vocabulary training, which emphasises repeated exposure to mathematical keywords, can enhance students' understanding and reduce barriers related to learning caused by a higher cognitive load due to language processing.

So, with all that in mind – how can we tackle these challenges effectively in our lessons? One method is the use of keyword flashcards. Each student has a keyring and then multiple cards (A7 or an eighth of A4 works well) and each time a keyword crops up, the teacher directs students to write it on their card. On one face the word, and on the reverse, the meaning or definition. This then becomes a quick easy bespoke set of flash cards. From this one resource, there are many different applications such as self-quizzing, peer quizzing, starting with the keyword and guess the definition or flip this and start with the definition and guess the keyword. Flashcards are an easy and highly effective tool for self-regulation, itself a key metacognitive element. Self-regulation strategies, including specifically quizzing using flashcards, correlate positively with higher academic achievement (Xu et al., 2021).

A second strategy that I love to do and is always popular with students is Mathematical Taboo. In this game, students must describe a word to a partner but not use any of the given 'taboo words'. An example is shown in Figure 7.1.

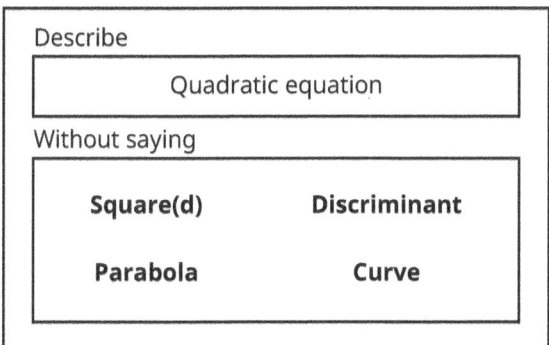

Figure 7.1 An example of a Mathematical Taboo card

The metacognitive power of this activity comes from the planning required to describe the keyword without relying on use of common terms. Students need to draw on a deeper understanding of the concept to plan and execute their explanation effectively. For an advanced variation, you can play 'Oobat' (Simply the reverse of Taboo). In Oobat, the describer must use all of the given words in their explanation. This is more challenging for the describer, as they have to integrate each word logically.

A successful explanation almost always leads to a correct guess, so it is important to rotate speakers frequently to maximise the learning impact. Figure 7.2 is an example of an Oobat card.

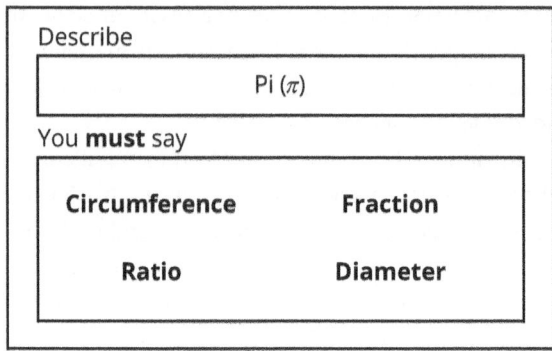

Figure 7.2   An example of an Oobat card

Here the desired outcome might sound something like: 'This is a number which cannot be expressed as a fraction. It is the ratio of a circle's circumference to its diameter.'

These activities not only support the retention of key vocabulary but also serve as a low-stakes, highly engaging way for students to practise strategic thinking and planning before they act – essential metacognitive skills. By requiring students to carefully consider how they describe or explain keywords, both Mathematical Taboo and Oobat encourage deeper cognitive processing, promoting a more robust understanding of mathematical language. Over time, these strategies can help students build confidence in using precise mathematical language, reduce anxiety around more challenging terms and, ultimately, enhance their overall problem-solving abilities.

Graphic organisers

The use of graphic organisers feels organic to mathematics due to the high number of diagrams, charts, and pictorial representations we naturally utilise as part of teaching our subject. Fuson et al. (2014) suggest that visual supports, such as graphic organisers, are essential tools for supporting deep learning in mathematics. There are many types of organisers, each with its own focus, but one type I have used with success is the Frayer model. A Frayer model is a simple four-section diagram primarily used to support vocabulary development and conceptual understanding. Its structured and consistent approach allows students to categorise Mathematical concepts, which can lead to improved problem-solving skills and reduce the likelihood of misconceptions. Figure 7.3 is an example of a Frayer model.

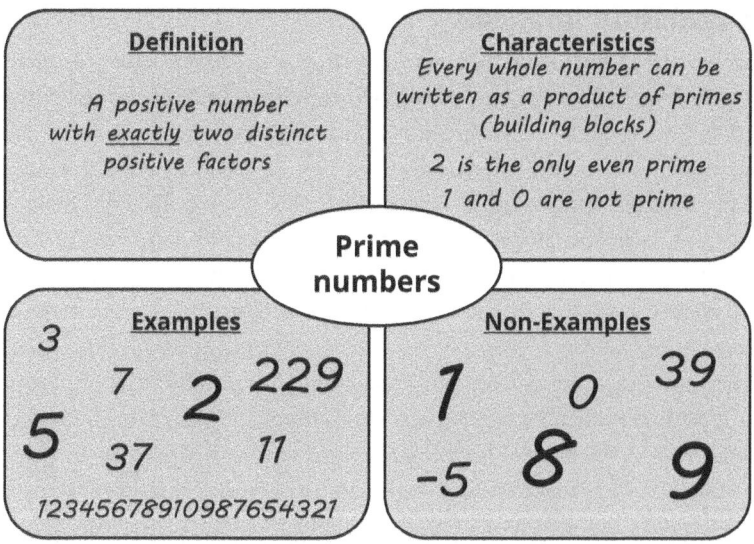

Figure 7.3 An example of a Frayer model

The above example is a simple but pivotal concept, which we know can give rise to plenty of early misconceptions. One of the strengths of the Frayer model is the inclusion of the non-examples section, which supports addressing these misconceptions in a safe way, ensuring that no unintended ones take root. For instance, consider how many students believe that one is a prime number. This misconception often arises from a poorly worded definition (e.g., 'a number that can be divided by one and itself'). The Frayer model allows us to provide a clear definition and follow up with key non-examples, further solidifying students' understanding and minimising the chances of an incorrect interpretation.

These models can be particularly useful as a planning tool for younger or less experienced students who are learning foundational steps in mathematics, where definitions of new concepts are plentiful. For example, when teaching prime factor decomposition, the value of a Frayer model for prime numbers becomes clear. It helps students plan effective responses to the task, activates prior knowledge and avoids common errors, such as considering one a prime factor. The Frayer model has many applications; it can later serve as a prompt for recall tasks and also acts as a focal point for group activities. By working together to fill out the Frayer model, students engage in discussions that promote meta-cognitive dialogue, allowing them to articulate their thought processes and reflect on their understanding. This collaboration helps them develop the inner monolog critical to met-acognitive thinking by practising and refining their ideas aloud with peers. Furthermore, the Frayer model has been shown to be particularly beneficial for students with diverse learning needs. Research indicates that graphic organisers, such as the Frayer model, can support vocabulary acquisition and understanding for students with disabilities, promoting inclusivity in mathematics education (Dazzeo & Rao, 2020).

Exam question analysis

Whether we agree with it or not, mathematics is a subject where proficiency and understanding are primarily assessed through terminal exams at various critical points in a student's education. It is, therefore, important that we do not shy away from exposing students to exam materials and settings. One way to develop students' metacognitive abilities when using these materials is by having them evaluate pre-completed exam questions. The nuance of this activity (and why it fits into the planning phase) is that students will follow it up by attempting a similarly structured question, planning ahead to integrate the successful aspects of the previously evaluated response.

In order to achieve the desired outcome from this activity, it is important not to confuse it with a multiple-choice question, where there are two incorrect answers and one correct as the desired learning outcomes are very different. In this exercise, present students with three correct responses to an exam question. Their task is to identify elements independent of the final solution that contribute to the overall quality of the answer. For example, consider these four correct solutions in which the responder has:

- Shown a lot of incorrect calculations and working before settling on the final answer, making the final answer unclear.
  (Focus on developing exam technique and layout)
- Provided little to no working but arrived at the correct final answer.
  (Focus on importance of showing all steps to avoid losing method marks)
- Taken an inefficient approach to solving the problem.
  (Focus on exam pace and demonstration of broader understanding)
- Used long decimal numbers to preserve accuracy instead of utilising exact values or using calculator memory functions.
  (Focus on understanding of accuracy, rounding, and calculator technique)

I typically choose three of these four general foci for students to evaluate and learn from, depending on the class and their specific learning priorities at the time. This activity works especially well as a group task, where students can explore and debate their ideas in smaller groups before presenting their findings to the whole class. The feedback can then be gathered and codified into a checklist or set of guidelines based on the students' discussion points.

What makes this activity particularly impactful is following it up with a similarly structured question, where students apply the guidelines they have created. For broader mathematical exam technique, this approach works well as a one-off lesson, ideally conducted about a week before an assessment. By engaging in these reflective discussions, students not only strengthen their ability to evaluate mathematical solutions to exam questions but also develop and practise essential metacognitive skills related to planning and evaluating. This activity is successful at equipping them with tools they can carry forward with them in their metacognitive toolkit.

Monitoring

The following strategies are concerned with monitoring.

Key questions

Often in mathematics, students encounter large, unstructured questions that require them to perform various mini calculations in order to gain the relevant information required to solve the problem. Sometimes, these questions are divided into more structured parts (a), (b), (c), etc., but this is not always the case, particularly as students transition into A Level mathematics. These types of questions can be intimidating to students and affect motivation and resilience, with a common challenge students face being knowing where and how to start. To help students approach these types of problems, we try to teach them a means-end methodology. Means-end analysis involves identifying the initial state (the problem) and the goal state (the solution) and then selecting an approach designed to reduce the difference between these states. This process is repeated until the initial gap becomes traversable, helping students break down complex problems into more manageable steps.

Consider this question

> *A and B are straight lines*
> *Line A has equation $2y - 5x - 3 = 0$*
> *Line B passes through the points $(10, -1)$ and $(1.5, 2.4)$*
> *Show that the lines are perpendicular to each other.*

There is quite a lot of mathematics here for students to identify and develop a means-end analysis approach. They could start with questions designed to reduce the difference between the initial state and the goal, such as:

- What is the relationship between perpendicular lines?
- How do I work out the gradient of Line A from an equation?
- How do I write line A in $y = mx + c$ form?
- How do I calculate the gradient from two given points?

Initially, this process should (understandably) be teacher-led while students are still in a relative novice state. However, paradoxically, once students begin to develop relative fluency with their domain knowledge, teachers should flip their instructional techniques. The expertise reversal effect, as discussed by Kalyuga et al. (2003), explains that as students' proficiency increases, instructional techniques that once supported novice learners can become significantly less effective or even counterproductive for expert learners. As students attain a good level of fluency and automaticity, they require more independent exploration and problem-solving applications. With this in mind, one effective approach for these learners is the use of goal-free problems. These are open-ended tasks where students explore a given situation without a specific question to answer. This metacognitive strategy is a game changer because it removes the pressure of achieving a predetermined solution and instead emphasises wider understanding of the topic.

Consider the previous question re-imagined as a goal-free problem.

A and B are straight lines
Line A has equation $2y - 5x - 3 = 0$
Line B passes through the points $(10, -1)$ and $(1.5, 2.4)$
Find out as much as you can about these lines.

A really powerful follow-up activity to further develop students' critical thinking is to ask them, 'What do you think the question could have been?' This encourages students to review their discovered information and construct thoughtful questions, ranging from simple one-step calculations to more detailed multi-step problem-solving questions.

The emphasis on process over product encourages students to engage with the material in a way that promotes critical thinking and conceptual understanding, both key metacognitive skills. The importance of these metacognitive skills in problem-solving cannot be overstated; Lan suggests that the use of goal-free problems can enhance these skills by allowing students to reflect on their thought processes without the pressure of achieving a predetermined outcome (Lan, 2020). Key questions can be a responsive part of a monitoring phase within a lesson; initially, this should be more teacher-led, but as the fluency and understanding of the students increase, the questions can be generated by the students themselves. Goal-free problems are a powerful way of cultivating this transition from teacher to student agency.

Warning signs

Encouraging students to self-monitor for warning signs can be a highly effective tool in developing both comprehension and metacognitive awareness. These warning signs can take the form of simple 'don't do this' guardrails, which by their nature tend to be more generalised:

- Do not forget units or forget to check you are using correct units.
- Do not round prematurely and check the accuracy required for the final answer.

Alternatively, they can manifest as more comprehensive, misconception-based self-regulation prompts, which require a higher level of conceptual understanding and are more specific:

- Do not forget to add two radii lengths when finding perimeter of sectors.
- Be careful to expand double brackets correctly and avoid $(x + 3)^2 = x^2 + 9$

We know from experience that all students (even their teachers!) can make mistakes. This is not inherently bad, as these errors, like non-examples in a Frayer model, provide valuable contrasts to affirmative examples of a concept. While mistakes are an inherent part of the learning process and the journey from novice to expert, it is understandable that we aim to eliminate them as students develop fluency and automaticity. One way to reduce the frequency of mistakes is by encouraging students to take a moment before beginning a task to reflect on potential issues. By identifying both general and specific warning signs that might arise, students are better prepared to avoid common pitfalls by monitoring themselves against these during the task.

It can be challenging to convey the value of metacognitive strategies when students are experiencing a high degree of success completing independent practice activities designed to build fluency. Students often think, 'I'm getting all of these correct, so why should I invest time in this thought process?'. On the surface, it is a fair question, and I address it by helping students understand that the pressure of an exam scenario cannot be replicated in the classroom or even in a mock exam. No matter how successful they are in class, it is always a lower-stakes environment compared to the final exam, where mistakes can occur due to the added pressure. Developing and practising planning and monitoring strategies, along with utilising the self-regulation needed to recognise early warning signs, helps students avoid going too far down the wrong path. This is especially important for long, unstructured questions, where these skills can be the difference between two grades. Additionally, it prevents students from wasting a significant portion of examination time on an incorrect strategy, which would otherwise increase pressure on the remainder of the exam, increasing the likelihood of further errors. With this context, students can better appreciate the importance of this approach.

Checklists

Checklists can be an effective scaffold for novice learners when tackling process heavy mathematics problems. Take, for example, solving quadratic inequalities, these types of questions require several sub-tasks to be completed in sequence before arriving at the final answer. To support my Year 11 students in mastering this process, I provided them with the following checklist:

Solving quadratic equations
1 Rearrange the inequality to have 0 on one side
2 Decide how to solve the inequality (Factorise? Formula? Complete the Square?)
3 Solve the inequality to find CV
4 SKETCH the graph
5 Shade the correct region
6 Write the inequality
7 Check values

When structuring this checklist, I aim for it to be prescriptive enough that students can use it as an effective monitoring tool at each sub-stage of the calculation. At the same time, I want it to be general enough so that students do not need to navigate multiple checklists for different variations of questions, hence the inclusion of step one, which may not always be necessary. The checklist helps students to develop and practise their inner dialogue (self-talk), which is a significant metacognitive strategy that can support their learning in mathematics. Research shows that developing an inner dialogue can enhance students' understanding of mathematical concepts, improve problem-solving skills, and promote self-regulation in learning (Choi et al., 2017). The structure of a checklist prompts students to mentally ask monitoring-based questions such as:

- 'What stage am I at now?'
- 'What should I do next?'
- 'Have I missed any steps?'

There are several useful extensions to this activity once students reach an appropriate level of domain knowledge mastery and begin to demonstrate fluency in their own metacognitive abilities. For instance, students can be asked to create their own checklists for a task. In theory, there should be very little deviation between checklists, making this activity well-suited for peer marking and feedback. Any discrepancies may reveal previously unknown misconceptions in students' thought processes, providing a powerful opportunity for the teacher to give targeted and impactful feedback. Another extension is to present students with incorrect or incomplete checklists and ask them to identify what is wrong or which key stages are missing from the process. This activity also holds significant value for the teacher as a non-traditional assessment tool by making students' thought sequences visible. By incorporating checklists, students not only refine their problem-solving strategies but also develop a deeper awareness of their own thought processes, enhancing their knowledge of self.

Evaluation

This section looks at metacognitive strategies for evaluation.

New strategy

Within mathematics, there are often multiple strategies to solve a given problem. For example, Pythagoras' theorem, one of the key formulae in GCSE mathematics, has an estimated 370 different proofs. Research suggests that relying on a limited repertoire of strategies can weaken students' problem-solving skills and hinder flexible thinking (Ramirez et al., 2016). This indicates that exposure to a broader range of approaches is essential for developing creative and evaluative mathematicians.

An effective way to develop students' metacognitive skills is by challenging them to discover new or alternative strategies for solving problems they have already encountered. Encouraging this type of exploration promotes deeper reflection on the problem-solving process and enhances their ability to evaluate and adapt their methods. However, it is important that students first secure a solid grasp of the initial strategies before exploring alternatives. Without this foundational understanding, the task may become overwhelming and potentially counterproductive.

Consider the solving of monic quadratic equations, where the equations are already presented as equal to zero, eliminating the need for rearrangement. Once students have developed a secure level of fluency with different solving methods (factorising, completing the square, and using the quadratic formula), metacognitive activities can be introduced as evaluative tools. We could present a monic quadratic equation on the board and ask students to solve it on a piece of paper without specifying which method to use. Often, students will instinctively default to the method they feel most comfortable with. After they have solved the equation and you have checked both their answers and, crucially, their method selection, ask them to solve the equation again using a different method, on a new sheet of paper. Repeat the process a third time, allowing students to tackle the problem using all three methods. Importantly, their work is preserved on separate sheets, helping them reflect on the differences between the methods.

These three solutions to the same monic quadratic equation then provide a valuable prompt for a rich evaluative discussion about the method selection. I would ask the following reflective questions to guide students in their evaluations:

- 'Why did you initially select this method?'
- 'After solving the equation, did you have any regrets about your initial method choice?'
- 'What are the strengths of the method you used?'
- 'Under what conditions might this method be less effective?'
- 'Are there any clues we can look for that help us choose the best method the first time?'

These questions encourage students to reflect not only on their own decision-making processes but also on the broader implications of their choices in Mathematics. This reflective practice can enhance their metacognitive skills and lead to a deeper understanding of mathematical concepts.

I have found this activity particularly useful for helping students evaluate the effectiveness and efficiency of their strategies at the end of a task. Engaging in this process consistently encourages students to become more reflective after solving problems, gradually influencing their thinking before they even begin. Over time, this reflection helps them develop the habit of selecting the most appropriate strategy from the outset, leading to more efficient and confident problem-solving.

Self/peer marking

Mathematics is unique compared to many other subjects because there is often (though not always) a clear right or wrong answer, with little room for nuance. As a result, when students engage in extensive independent practice, it generates a large volume of work to be marked. Teachers often feel obligated to perform 'tick-and-flick' marking, simply acknowledging that the work has been completed successfully. While this type of marking can boost motivation by giving students recognition, it does little to develop their understanding. Given the time constraints and workload on teachers, it is far more impactful to allocate time to supporting students who are getting things wrong, rather than ticking through 400 questions from students who are getting it all correct. Do not get me wrong, there are clear benefits to students receiving affirmation that you value their hard work and you know they are doing well, but this can be done in many other less time-consuming ways such as whole class feedback.

By incorporating self- and peer-marking alongside live feedback, we can achieve a balance that both motivates students and fosters metacognitive development. After a task, share the answers and give students time to mark their work. Following this, and with a front-loaded prompt, allocate additional time for students to *think* about the specific feedback they will give, but with no writing. This thinking time encourages deeper engagement with the feedback process, helping to avoid shallow responses.

The process of giving and receiving feedback, whether written or oral, can significantly enhance students' critical thinking and analytical skills. By evaluating their peers' work, students learn to identify strengths and weaknesses in Mathematical reasoning, which can, in turn, improve their own problem-solving abilities. Peer feedback routines expose students to a variety of perspectives on Mathematical concepts and strategies, deepening their understanding (Mon & Zein, 2017). This repeated exposure and practice strengthens their metacognitive skills, particularly the wider 'knowledge of cognition' element.

I recommend starting with peer feedback and gradually transitioning to self-feedback. When students provide feedback to peers, there is a natural obligation to offer meaningful insights, which may not be as strong with initial attempts at self-assessment. Peer feedback helps students develop the ability to evaluate and critique effectively in a specific domain before turning that critical eye to their own work. Scaffolding this process with examples or non-examples can further support their growth. For instance, banning empty phrases like 'good work', 'well done', or 'nice presentation' shifts the focus from minor motivational gains to deeper learning and metacognitive reflection.

Good, better, and best answers

We all know that, by far, the best investment any department can make (outside of purchasing this book, of course!) is buying a set of mini whiteboards for each classroom. They are simply the best assessment tool available and the catalyst for effective adaptive teaching. While we use them extensively in mathematics, they are not exclusive to the subject. There are many effective ways to utilise mini whiteboards in any lesson, instantly generating a class-wide set of responses that can be assessed almost immediately, leading to highly responsive teaching and feedback.

This tool can also serve as a fantastic opportunity to enhance students' metacognitive development. The best time to do this exercise is when a level of mastery has been achieved, and the procedural content knowledge is secure. Let us assume that students are using whiteboards to solve a multifaceted problem without a clear and immediate solution. As students are already highly proficient in this area, you anticipate a high rate of correct answers. However, typically within a proportion of correct answers, there are likely to be a range of good, better, and best responses. These might be differentiated by the layout, exam technique, lack of diagrams, or the strategy selected. You can collect a few of these correct solutions with differing strategies, display them to the class, label them A, B, and C and engage the class in a discussion comparing the approaches used, ultimately agreeing on a good, better and best answer. To deepen students' metacognitive abilities, it is important to focus not on the content (the correctness) but on evaluating the strengths and weaknesses of each method selected. This approach facilitates a rich evaluative discussion, where students can articulate their understanding and justify their rankings.

Let us look at an example from an A Level lesson that generated three correct, but distinct, responses (see Figure 7.4).

Question: Consider a geometric series with first term a and common ratio 2 and a second geometric series with first term b and common ratio 5.

Show that $a = \frac{52}{5}b$

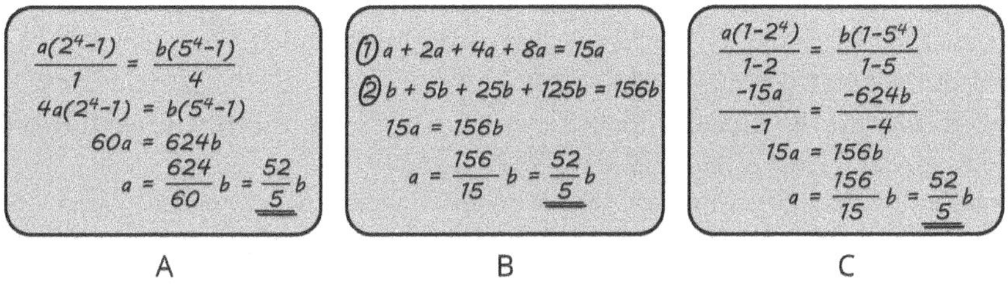

A

$$\frac{a(2^4-1)}{1} = \frac{b(5^4-1)}{4}$$
$$4a(2^4-1) = b(5^4-1)$$
$$60a = 624b$$
$$a = \frac{624}{60}b = \frac{52}{5}b$$

B

$$① \; a + 2a + 4a + 8a = 15a$$
$$② \; b + 5b + 25b + 125b = 156b$$
$$15a = 156b$$
$$a = \frac{156}{15}b = \frac{52}{5}b$$

C

$$\frac{a(1-2^4)}{1-2} = \frac{b(1-5^4)}{1-5}$$
$$\frac{-15a}{-1} = \frac{-624b}{-4}$$
$$15a = 156b$$
$$a = \frac{156}{15}b = \frac{52}{5}b$$

Figure 7.4 Three responses to the question

In this case, all students arrived at the correct answer, so the focus shifts from content accuracy to a deeper evaluation of method selection, specifically its relative strengths and weaknesses. This analysis opens up a rich discussion where students can articulate their understanding of what makes an answer strong and, crucially, why it qualifies as such.

In the example above, I presented the problem after introducing the formula for the sum of a geometric series to n terms. Most students chose an approach similar to A or C and were surprised at how quickly I solved it (My whiteboard was approach B). In the ensuing evaluation, we discussed that while approach A was effective and better than C, given that the common ratio was greater than 1, approach B was ultimately the best due to its efficiency. Students identified that it required fewer calculations, thus reducing the likelihood of error. Nearly all students initially missed this simpler approach, which can be a common trend among high-ability students who are often eager to start calculating immediately without pausing to assess and plan their strategy through a metacognitive lens. This led to a discussion about how minor adjustments in their initial thought process could help them recognise alternative, efficient strategies in the future.

References

Bringula, R. P., Reguyal, J. J., Tan, D. D., & Ulfa, S. (2021). Mathematics self-concept and challenges of learners in an online learning environment during covid-19 pandemic. *Smart Learning Environments, 8*(1). https://doi.org/10.1186/s40561-021-00168-5

Choi, J., Walters, A. M., & Hoge, P. (2017). Self-reflection and math performance in an online learning environment. *Online Learning, 21*(4). https://doi.org/10.24059/olj.v21i4.1249

Dazzeo, R. & Rao, K. (2020). Digital Frayer model: Supporting vocabulary acquisition with technology and UDL. *TEACHING Exceptional Children, 53*(1), 34–42. https://doi.org/10.1177/0040059920911951

Fuson, K. C., Murata, A., & Abrahamson, D. (2014). Using learning path research to balance mathematics education. *The Oxford Handbook of Numerical Cognition*, 1036–1054. https://doi.org/10.1093/oxfordhb/9780199642342.013.003

Geary, D. C. (2012). *Folk knowledge and academic learning.* In *Encyclopaedia of the Sciences of Learning* (pp. 1305–1310). https://doi.org/10.1007/978-1-4419-1428-6_487

Huang, Y. Y., & Chou, H. (2024). EMI vocabulary support in high school mathematics: A quasiexperimental study in Taiwan. *International Journal of TESOL Studies, 6*(2), 43–60. https://doi.org/10.58304/ijts.20240204

Kalyuga, S., Ayres, P., Chandler, P., & Sweller, J. (2003). The expertise reversal effect. *Educational Psychologist, 38*, 23–31.

Kramarski, B. (2008). Promoting teachers' algebraic reasoning and self-regulation with metacognitive guidance. *Metacognition Learning, 3*, 83–99.https://doi.org/10.1007/s11409-008-9020-6

Lan, N. T. H. (2020). Metacognitive skills with mathematical problem-solving of secondary school students in Vietnam - a case study. *Universal Journal of Educational Research, 8*(12A), 7461–7478. https://doi.org/10.13189/ujer.2020.082530

Mon, Y. Y., & Zein, S. (2017). Effective use of peer-feedback in developing academic writing skills of undergraduate students. *Language Education in Asia, 8*(2), 176–191. https://doi.org/10.5746/leia/17/v8/i2/a04/mon_zein

Pate, M. L., & Miller, G. (2011). Effects of regulatory self-questioning on secondary level students' problem-solving performance. *Journal of Agricultural Education, 52*(1), 72–84. https://doi.org/10.5032/jae.2011.01072

Ramirez, G., Chang, H., Maloney, E. A., Levine, S. C., & Beilock, S. L. (2016). On the relationship between math anxiety and math achievement in early elementary school: The role of problem solving strategies. *Journal of Experimental Child Psychology, 141*, 83–100. https://doi.org/10.1016/j.jecp.2015.07.014

Slusser, E., Ribner, A., & Shusterman, A. (2018). Language counts: Early language mediates the relationship between parent education and children's math ability. *Developmental Science, 22*(3). https://doi.org/10.1111/desc.12773

Susanto, A., Dafik, D., & Prastiti, T. D. (2023). The activities framework on project-based learning: The use of autodesk sketchbook to improve students' metacognition thinking skills in solving polygon tessellation problems. *International Journal of Research Publication and Reviews, 4*(6), 1986–1997. https://doi.org/10.55248/gengpi.4.623.45803

Temel, S. (2013). Prospective chemistry teachers' problem solving achievement according to their levels of metacognitive skills. *Problems of Education in the 21st Century, 51*(1), 126–131. https://doi.org/10.33225/pec/13.51.126

Xu, J., Ong, J., Tran, T., Kollar, Y., Wu, A., Vujicic, M., & Hsiao, H. (2021). *The Impact of Study and Learning Strategies on Post-Secondary Student Academic Achievement: A Mixed-Methods Systematic Review.* https://doi.org/10.31234/osf.io/7ng5y

8

Science

David Boyce

Introduction

Guiding learners to focus on their own thinking offers benefits across all subjects, but nowhere is this more transformative than in the sciences. Science seeks to reveal truths hidden beneath the surface, relying on observation, experimentation and analysis to uncover what we cannot immediately see. The study of science is intricate, challenging learners to engage with concepts that are subtle, invisible or abstract. This complexity demands more than straightforward explanations; science teaching must bring these ideas to life, making the unseen, accessible and the abstract tangible.

To achieve this, skilled science teachers rely on a varied toolkit of instructional strategies designed to engage students' imaginations and promote deeper, more critical thinking. Techniques such as using models to represent complex ideas, drawing analogies to make difficult concepts relatable and breaking down ideas mathematically to reveal their underlying principles all serve as pathways into understanding. However, these techniques can sometimes be met with resistance from learners, who may find the methods unfamiliar or challenging.

The most effective way to address this resistance is to explain the reasoning behind each approach. By making the purpose of these strategies clear – that understanding one concept can illuminate another – teachers help students see the value in these methods. Over time, this approach fosters an open-mindedness and a readiness in learners to engage with even the most abstract concepts and techniques. This way, students not only grasp scientific content but also become more adaptable thinkers, capable of embracing various methods to reach understanding.

Mastering science goes beyond grasping challenging concepts; it demands the practical application of skills and techniques. To excel in science, students must not only understand theoretical ideas but also be able to carry out experiments methodically, apply calculations accurately and clearly communicate their findings and reasoning both in exams and in broader scientific discussions.

In this exploration, we delve into nine specific metacognitive techniques that can significantly enhance learners' scientific capabilities. These techniques help students reflect on their own thinking, develop strategies to approach complex tasks and build the confidence to tackle scientific problems effectively. By integrating these metacognitive strategies into their study practices, learners can strengthen their ability to apply scientific knowledge with precision, work through calculations with accuracy and present their ideas coherently. Together, these skills build a strong foundation not only for exam success but also for a deeper engagement with science as a discipline.

Problem-solving grids

This grid provides a structured framework to guide pupils' thought processes throughout a task, making explicit what they should be considering at each stage. It serves as a valuable tool for prompting learners to engage in purposeful reflection, encouraging them to think critically and methodically as they work through each part of the task.

In practice, students begin by completing the first three boxes in the grid, which are labelled 'comprehension,' 'connections,' and 'strategies'. The comprehension box prompts them to ensure they fully understand the task requirements and any key concepts. In the connections box, students are encouraged to link the task to prior knowledge or relevant information, fostering a broader understanding and helping them to contextualise what they are learning. The strategies box then guides students to identify and plan effective approaches or methods to tackle the task. These steps collectively prepare pupils to approach the task with clarity and purpose.

After completing these initial sections, students move on to perform the task itself. Once the task is completed, they return to the grid to fill in the final box, 'evaluation'. Here, they assess the effectiveness of their approach, reflect on what worked well and consider any adjustments they might make in future. This evaluative step encourages students to think critically about their process and fosters a habit of self-improvement.

Using this grid throughout the task not only structures pupils' thinking but also enhances their metacognitive awareness, equipping them with valuable skills to manage and assess their own learning more effectively (Table 8.1)

Table 8.1   A problem-solving grid

Comprehension	Connection
What is the task asking you to do?	When have you encountered a similar problem?
What are the key works in the task?	What is the same and what is different?
What relevant information have you been provided with and how may this help?	How will your evaluation from the connected task help you in this task?
Strategies	**Evaluation**
What are the different strategies that I can use to complete this task?	What went well, and how do you know?
	Was your strategy choice effective?
How do they vary in their utility?	Have you met the task criteria?
What are their relative strengths and weaknesses?	What would you do differently next time?

.

A useful illustration of cognitive load issues in science education can be found in the framing of a required practical for A-level sciences. Typically, students are provided with a set of written instructions outlining each stage of the experiment. These instructions are often highly detailed, breaking down each task into specific steps that guide the student through the experiment. While this detailed guidance is intended to ensure procedural accuracy, it can inadvertently create a barrier to deeper understanding, particularly for those less familiar with the experimental context.

The problem lies in the level of specificity in these instructions, which are usually designed for step-by-step adherence. Such detail, although helpful for technical precision, can overwhelm students' working memory, making it difficult for them to conceptualise the broader scientific objectives behind the practical. Working memory has a limited capacity, so students focused on executing each step may struggle to simultaneously process the 'big picture' – the connections to underlying theories, the purpose of each step or how the findings relate to broader scientific concepts.

This issue highlights a key challenge in practical science education: balancing procedural guidance with opportunities for students to engage with the experiment's purpose and implications. When learners are overly focused on following instructions meticulously, they may find it harder to develop independent scientific thinking, limiting their ability to analyse, reflect, and fully understand the experiment's goals. Effective framing of these practicals could therefore include structured guidance that introduces stages of reflection, prompting students to think critically about why each step is necessary and how it connects to the overall scientific enquiry, thereby reducing cognitive load and enhancing meaningful learning.

The development of the seminar method for teaching experimental physics in the early 1960s (Conway et al., 1963) was a response to concerns over the limitations of traditional physics instruction. To counteract low engagement with practicals, the seminar method emerged, emphasising structured, yet flexible, discussion and hands-on engagement in experimental processes. This method aimed to move away from passive learning towards a more active, engaging environment, by prioritising student involvement.

Building on this and other works, Adam Boxer has developed an approach called the Slow Practical, which goes further in addressing cognitive load and maintaining engagement in science practicals. Boxer's (2018) approach segments each practical task into manageable steps. The teacher demonstrates each stage of the experiment, allowing students to focus on one element at a time. This breakdown reduces the likelihood of cognitive overload and ensures students can concentrate on understanding and safely executing each component without becoming overwhelmed by multiple steps at once. In this way, Boxer's approach not only organises but also enhances the learning experience by allowing students to internalise each part of the process fully.

The Slow Practical method revitalises practical science teaching, tackling the long-standing issue of student disengagement. By showing each step, addressing potential misconceptions and encouraging questions, this approach turns the practical lesson into an interactive and purposeful experience. The result is a more focused, organised classroom environment where students work with increased clarity and confidence. This method offers a modern, effective solution to the criticisms raised decades ago, providing today's students with a structured framework that allows them to learn experimental physics in a systematic, effective, and engaging way.

In my teaching, I use a metacognitive approach combined with student responses to help them internalise practical instructions effectively. Rather than halting the class at intervals, I start by giving a step-by-step demonstration, prompting them to think about what they need to observe and consider at each stage. As I go through each step, I ask questions that draw out the essential aspects they need to keep in mind – such as observations they should make, accuracy, safety considerations, and the experimental skills they will need. This helps students understand the deeper reasoning behind each part of the practical.

Once we have gone through the demonstration, I repeat the process, this time using a mime-based approach with limited verbal instructions. During this second round, I keep the steps simple – just actions like 'Place this here', 'Mix' or 'Heat'. These simplified motions serve as memory markers, giving students reference points that are easy to remember without overloading their working memory. Each action serves as a place-holder that connects back to the full explanation, helping them recall the sequence without getting lost in details.

Finally, I ask the students to guide me through the steps, and I mime their instructions as they recall each part of the process. I pause along the way to prompt them to explain the reasoning behind each step, encouraging them to think about why it is done that way and what considerations are needed. This method allows them to link each memory marker to its underlying purpose and concepts, helping them retain both the procedural flow and the detailed knowledge required for accuracy, safety, and understanding.

Reflecting on these questions encourages metacognition, helping pupils not only understand what the task requires but also think critically about how they approach it. By engaging in metacognitive practices, such as identifying key terms and recognising relevant information, students gain a clearer sense of the task's overarching learning objectives. This self-awareness, or metacognition, allows them to connect the current experiment to prior experiences, enhancing their ability to apply useful strategies from past tasks. Through evaluating their strategies' strengths and weaknesses, students practice metacognitive reflection, assessing which approaches are most effective and why. Ultimately, this consistent focus on metacognition enables students to become more adaptable and thoughtful experimenters, using each learning experience to refine and improve their scientific skills.

Exam question analysis

Mark schemes for long-answer questions are typically crafted with a teacher in mind. They are often written in technical shorthand or abbreviated notes to avoid overloading the marker's working memory. However, when this unedited, context-free information is handed directly to pupils with the expectation that they will simply 'learn the right answers', it creates a significant skills gap. This approach overlooks the fact that students require more context and guidance to interpret the mark scheme effectively.

A more effective method, one that incorporates analysis and higher-order meta-cognitive skills, is to have pupils study a variety of well-crafted long-answer question responses. By examining different high-quality examples, students can see the same key information presented repeatedly, often phrased in slightly different ways, but each one aiming to convey the same core ideas. This repetition not only reinforces the essential content but also allows pupils to go beyond simply checking off required points; it encourages them to gain an understanding of the examiner's perspective. By critically analysing what an examiner might be looking for, students can reflect on their own approach to answering questions, refining their ability to structure and present information effectively. This metacognitive process shifts their focus from 'Did I include everything?' to 'How can I better convey my understanding to meet the examiner's expectations?'

Strategy evaluation

A teacher who remembers the challenges of mastering foundational tasks and incorporates strategies from their own learning journey is often seen as particularly effective. At first glance, the formula triangle may seem like an ingenious shortcut, and indeed, its application goes beyond the basic distance, speed, and time formula. It can also be used for a variety of other equations, such as those for momentum, magnification, and molar mass, making it appear incredibly versatile and useful.

However, the drawback of the formula triangle is that it provides a solution without fostering an understanding of the underlying principles. This approach is purely procedural; no matter how many times it is used, it does not contribute to a genuine conceptual grasp of the material. Instead, it simply offers a quick way to rearrange formulas, often bypassing the deeper understanding necessary for true mastery of the subject.

Pupils are naturally drawn to using the formula triangle – it seems to work for all the initial problems they face, and it is repetitive, straightforward use appears too beneficial to ignore. This creates a challenge for the teacher, who wants to teach the underlying skills that the formula triangle bypasses. The teacher is then faced with the task of encouraging pupils to adopt a different approach, even though they have already experienced success with the formula triangle. This can feel like a struggle between introducing a deeper understanding and the pupils' attachment to a strategy they find easy and reliable.

A teacher could use the metacognitive strategy evaluation to help pupils move away from the formula triangle by guiding them through a comparison of different problem-solving approaches. The teacher might begin by modelling several methods for rearranging and applying formulas, including traditional algebraic manipulation alongside the formula triangle. Through questioning and discussion, the teacher could encourage pupils to explore the relative strengths and weaknesses of each approach.

For instance, the teacher might ask pupils to identify situations where the formula triangle works well but highlight cases where it could fall short, such as in more complex problems requiring a deeper understanding of variable relationships. By examining the purpose and limitations of each method, pupils can start to see the formula triangle as a useful shortcut but not necessarily the most effective strategy for more complex work. Through this reflective process, pupils are encouraged to think critically about their approach, ultimately guiding them to choose methods that foster a more robust understanding and improve the accuracy and efficiency of their problem-solving.

Checklists

In his work on responding to long-answer questions, Jones (2022) advocates for a 'stepping stone' approach to constructing extended responses. He likens the process of addressing each bullet point to stepping out into a fast-flowing river. At each step, students are encouraged to ask themselves, 'What do I need to do next?' This technique effectively creates a metacognitive checklist, guiding students through the response process.

By using this method, students can assess their progress within their answers, ensuring they thoroughly address all components of the question before reaching a conclusion. This approach helps prevent premature endings to their responses, promoting a more comprehensive and well-structured answer overall.

I employ a similar approach, but with the added twist of encouraging learners to create their own prompts derived from the command statements present in the question. For instance, most six-mark questions typically provide several prompts designed to help ensure they address all aspects of the question.

Building on the idea of stepping stones, students can check off each prompt as they tackle it, which serves as a visual and mental guide throughout their response. This method allows them to maintain their momentum, ensuring they transition smoothly from one part of the question to the next. They continue this process until every aspect of the question has been thoroughly addressed, thereby fostering a sense of completion and ensuring a comprehensive response.

Another significant advantage of using a checklist or the stepping stone approach is that it provides learners with a mental framework that aids in visualising their answers. This framework encourages them to respond to the question in a logical and coherent sequence. Just as stepping stones must be taken in the correct order to safely cross a river, students should also follow a structured path when formulating their responses.

If students attempt to address the parts of a question out of order, it can lead to confusion and a lack of clarity in their answers. In an examination context, adhering to a logical sequence is particularly crucial, as examiners often award higher marks for responses that are well-structured and methodically organised. By following this approach, learners not only enhance their understanding of the question but also improve the overall quality of their responses, thereby increasing their chances of achieving better grades.

Task success criteria

Thirty years ago, Key Stage 3 (KS3) science practicals followed a rigid format designed to prepare students for GCSE coursework. A typical write-up included a hypothesis, a detailed method with a diagram, results in a table or graph and a conclusion with an evaluation. While this approach aimed to instil good scientific practice, it often felt forced and did not always foster genuine engagement.

Today, many educators see this method as outdated. Instead, they prefer assessing understanding through reflective questions after the practical. Some even argue against practicals altogether, suggesting students benefit more from focussing on the concepts behind the experiments.

This shift has led many schools to convert science labs into traditional classrooms, reducing the need for costly lab benches. A 'lab swap' system allows classes to use a shared lab for experiments. However, making practical work less accessible risks disengaging students and limiting hands-on learning, which is vital for understanding scientific principles. Balancing practical activities with meaningful engagement remains essential.

So, what is the point of practical activity and should you share success criteria for a practical experiment with the learners before or after the experiment? At a previous school, I had a headmaster observe a science lesson during a practical activity. He questioned a pupil, asking, 'Why are you doing this experiment?' He then added, 'There is no point in you doing this if you don't know what you are going to learn from it.' The headmaster did not know the first thing about science and he made it obvious every time he spoke.

Rarely do we conduct experiments to learn something specific, and even less frequently do we know what that specific learning is beforehand. If that were the goal, there would be little justification for carrying out the experiment. Often, we are looking at how an idea can be demonstrated. If this statement is true, how do we know it is true? Through this process, we develop experimental skills, build confidence, and deepen understanding of the scientific method, creating lasting memories that surpass those from simpler tasks like cut-and-stick activities. It is beneficial for students to be aware of this, so they are clear about why we approach things in this manner. The philosophy behind experimentation is important to share, even when you want the results of a particular experiment to be a surprise.

Rather than pursuing the more simplistic objective of 'finding out what happens when...', learners could take on the role of verifying established scientific principles. A fundamental aspect of science is its repeatability – the idea that scientific concepts and results can be consistently demonstrated through experiment. By taking on this verifying role, students engage with the idea that their skill as a scientist is not only about conducting an experiment but also about being able to replicate the results of other scientists reliably.

This process allows them to critically evaluate the evidence, understand why the results can be trusted and appreciate how those results support broader scientific theories. Importantly, this approach shifts the focus from simply completing a set of instructions to actively engaging with the principles behind the experiment.

To achieve this, learners must approach the practical work with greater mindfulness and metacognition – thinking not just about what they are doing but also about why they are doing it and how their actions contribute to verifying the scientific ideas. This deeper level of engagement helps foster critical thinking, enhances their understanding of the scientific method and develops their ability to evaluate experimental results effectively.

Flow maps

If science could be united by a single concept, it would be energy. Energy is, in some way, responsible for most of the phenomena we observe across the three branches of science. Despite being such a fundamental idea, it is quite challenging to define precisely what energy is. No words can adequately capture its essence. The best analogy I can think of is that energy serves as the currency of the Universe; it enables change and without it, nothing can transform. Our understanding of money follows a flow-like structure: we can hold cash, invest it in property, make bank transfers or incur debt. Wealth transitions from one form to another. Similarly, energy operates in a flow, and understanding this flow is often more important than pinpointing exactly what energy is.

Energy is relational, meaning students only begin to comprehend it by observing its effects on other objects and systems. It is valuable to share this perspective with learners, as it can be difficult to grasp. Viewing energy as an extensive, interconnected structure – rather than as a simple, isolated entity – provides a clearer understanding.

Drawing energy flow diagrams, which visually represent the relationships between energy stores and transfers, can help clarify and organise a learner's thinking. These diagrams allow students to contextualise each component of the system. At Key Stages 2 and 3, energy flows are often depicted as simple, linear diagrams with limited options. As students progress through Key Stages 4 and 5, these diagrams can become more complex, incorporating multiple energy inputs and outputs, and exploring both wasted and useful energy.

At Key Stages 4 and Key Stages 5, these diagrams can also be used numerically to represent the relative quantities of useful versus wasted energy, serving as visual representations of efficiency. The Sankey diagram is a key example of this: a fully quantitative scale diagram that illustrates all the energies involved. It is a versatile tool, applicable to any energy system, whether analysing a closed mechanical system or evaluating the metabolic efficiency of an organism like a jellyfish.

Warning signs

Making predictions is a fundamental part of science, as it serves as a test for any scientific theory. For a theory to be considered true, it must make predictions that can be verified through experiment. When a student conducts an experiment in a school science lab, they may begin by forming a hypothesis, making a prediction and designing an experiment to test if that prediction is correct. However, in most cases, with the experiment explained by the teacher, learning objectives displayed on the wall and success criteria provided beforehand, surprises are rare. Most students are able to predict the outcome of an experiment simply by following the teacher's guidance. In such situations, they often learn more from the shared goals of the activity than from the activity itself.

A skilled teacher can guide students to the edge of their current understanding and ask them to predict what will happen next. If designed effectively, the situation can be used to diagnose misconceptions about basic concepts. For instance, when teaching circuits and explaining how current and voltage behave in series and parallel circuits, I would ask students to predict what would happen to the current if an additional branch were added to a parallel circuit. A common response might be that the current would divide, with some flowing one way and some the other. But the follow-up question is: what happens to the current flowing through the battery? The correct answer is that the current increases, as adding another branch lowers the total resistance of the circuit and increases the current proportionally. Many students hold the misconception that the total current is fixed and cannot increase, particularly when another component is added. How a student responds to this prompt provides valuable insight for the teacher.

Red flags arise when a student struggles to make a simple prediction. For example, if a student can tell you the number of protons and neutrons in carbon but not in oxygen, it suggests that they may be relying on what they know about one specific case but are unable to apply that knowledge to make predictions about similar situations. It is important for students to understand that learning, much like science, involves testing their predictions and adapting their understanding based on new information.

Self/peer marking

Much of the declarative knowledge in science can be assessed using simple short-answer questions, where responses are often clearly right or wrong. Learners can quickly determine whether an answer is correct without necessarily knowing the answer themselves. This process serves as a useful metacognitive strategy, allowing them to identify the correct answer and differentiate it from incorrect ones rapidly.

It is more important for students to understand what can go wrong and why certain answers are incorrect than to simply verify whether their own answer is right. If learning has taken place, they should be able to recognise this independently. If it has not, peer marking can be a helpful initial intervention to help them catch up.

Since peer and self-marking involve metacognition, they offer advantages as learning strategies over teacher marking, which does not engage metacognitive processes. However, teacher marking can be more beneficial when the answers are nuanced, detailed and when determining correctness is challenging.

Learning diaries

At the end of the day, a teacher cannot do everything. It does not matter if they are the best in the field – if the learner makes no effort to engage with what they have been taught, progress will be limited. A skilled teacher can indeed inspire a greater proportion of pupils to aim high, becoming masters of motivation as well as subject expertise. But without the pupil's own desire to succeed, it remains an uphill struggle. Success in education takes many forms, and one outcome more valuable than exam results is a learner who takes pride in their knowledge and develops a genuine curiosity for the subject.

Our role as educators has two key aims: firstly, to raise the scientific literacy of all our pupils; and secondly, to provide the inspiration, expert instruction and encouragement needed to cultivate the next generation of specialists. There are many strategies to support motivated learners, but one of the most powerful is to encourage them to take pride in their knowledge and actively seek to expand it. A learning diary, where they can record and reflect on what they have learnt, is something I always encourage and take an interest in. I think of Galileo and Newton, whose work began as logs of exploration – seeking new discoveries or learning from the ideas of others. A lifelong quest for knowledge often starts with a journal.

When I was twelve, I developed an interest in the night sky and started recording my observations and discoveries in an exercise book. With childlike wonder, I documented my first sighting of Saturn's rings, a lunar eclipse and a comet travelling across the sky from starfield to starfield. When I received my first chemistry set, I wrote down every-thing I did and learnt with great attention to detail. Even as an adult, I continue to be a meticulous note-taker, often writing down anything I find interesting or do not yet know.

Now, as a teacher, I run an extracurricular astronomy club. Each year, when a new group of students arrives, I share my little thirty-year-old notebook filled with obser-vations, and the impact is profound – everyone wants one. There is nothing more fundamental to forming a scientific identity than having a journal in which you record your discoveries.

For a young scientist, a learning diary is an excellent metacognitive tool. It allows them to review and assess what they already know, explore their interests, and identify areas they want to learn more about.

Conclusion

Metacognition is a tool that supports learners throughout their educational journey, whether to maximise the value of practical experiments, grasp challenging and abstract concepts or excel in their studies. Understanding their own thinking, along with strategies that make learning more effective, richer and deeper, leads to better outcomes and more fulfilled, happier learners.

References

Boxer, A. (2018, December 6). *achemicalorthodoxy*. https://achemicalorthodoxy.co.uk/2018/12/06/the-slow-practical/

Conway, R. G., Mendoza, E., & Read, F. H. (1963). The seminar method of teaching experimental physics. *Physics Bulletin, 14*(12), 330.

Jones, G. (2022, August 3). *e=mc2andallthat*. https://physicsteacher.blog/2022/08/03/helping-students-with-extended-writing-questions-in-science/

9
English

Sarah Dowey

Introduction

Applying metacognition to the teaching of English can often feel challenging. This is partly because metacognition is a complex and abstract concept that can be difficult to define, making it susceptible to misinterpretation, especially in classroom settings. Additionally, while research into the educational benefits of metacognitive strategies has grown significantly (Quigley et al., 2018), there are still relatively few studies conducted in real classroom environments by qualified, specialist teachers, rather than by academic researchers (Perry et al., 2021). Of the available studies, many have focused on the application of metacognition in STEM subjects, leaving its potential impact in humanities subjects – particularly English – largely unexplored. This gap in research has left English somewhat neglected in the broader conversation about metacognitive learning. Furthermore, even where studies have examined metacognitive approaches, the findings on their impact on learning outcomes have been inconsistent (Motteram et al., 2016) and do not always demonstrate promising results (Gascoine et al., 2022).

This does not mean that metacognitive approaches cannot be successfully applied in the English classroom. In fact, cognitive processes naturally align with the way students learn. As part of my research into applying cognitive science strategies in English literature lessons (Dowey, 2023), I used a number of strategies, which I found helped scholars develop metacognitive thinking and improved my pedagogy. Relatively few of these strategies will be unfamiliar to you – I'm not trying to re-invent the wheel! Instead, I've selected techniques that work well when used through a metacognitive lens to help scholars become more aware of their learning processes and think more critically about how they learn. Finally, as with all cognitive and metacognitive strategies, the key to really making them work in the classroom, is clear exemplification through structured verbal modelling/'think alouds', so that scholars understand how an expert learner approaches the tasks.

Planning

Let's start by exploring strategies to support planning in the English classroom.

Graphic organisers: Frayer model

Graphic organisers are an effective tool to support scholars organise their ideas and develop their understanding of key English concepts and disciplinary knowledge. They can also be particularly powerful when paired with principles from Dual Coding Theory (Clark & Paivio, 1991), which suggests that combining verbal and visual information can enhance memory and understanding. While a wide range of graphic organisers can be effectively employed in the English classroom, this section will specifically focus on the use of Frayer Models and Mind Maps. These tools offer powerful, visual frameworks for supporting students' cognitive and metacognitive engagement with key concepts, particularly in the development of disciplinary knowledge and vocabulary. By examining these two approaches in depth, we can better understand how they facilitate deeper learning, encourage critical thinking, and promote meaningful connections across texts, ideas, and language structures.

The Frayer Model is a graphic organiser designed to help students build a deeper understanding of vocabulary by breaking down a word or concept into key components. It encourages active, metacognitive engagement with new terms by requiring learners to define, describe, and apply their understanding. Although several variations on the 4-part model exist (other sections can include: non-examples, characteristics, antonyms and links) the sections below (as shown in Figure 9.1) are particularly useful in promoting a metacognitive approach.

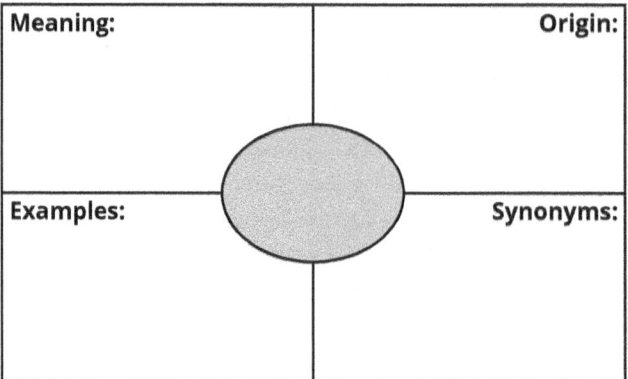

Figure 9.1 Frayer model template

Below are suggested stages that could be used to support scholars to complete each section, exemplified through the word 'subjugate'.

1 Meaning
   It might seem counterintuitive, but I generally advise against having scholars fill in definitions independently by looking them up in a dictionary. There are a few reasons for this. First, dictionary definitions can be difficult to navigate, especially when a word has multiple meanings or is explained using unfamiliar terms that only

add to scholars' confusion. More importantly, simply copying a definition doesn't guarantee genuine understanding – scholars may go through the motions without truly thinking about the word, which means they're not building a solid foundation for long-term retention. Instead, a more effective, metacognitive approach is to activate scholars' prior knowledge to help them construct meaningful mental models. This can be done through quick, targeted questioning or whole-class feedback using mini-whiteboards.

For example, you might ask:

○ Who knows what this word means?
○ What does this word make you think of?
○ What other words begin with the prefix 'sub'?
○ What does the prefix 'sub' mean?

By encouraging scholars to connect the new term with existing knowledge, you support deeper, more durable learning.

2   Origin

Storytelling is a powerful tool for helping learners retain information because it engages both cognitive and emotional processes, activates pattern recognition, and fosters meaningful connections that strengthen memory and understanding. Exploring a word's etymology with scholars is, in essence, uncovering the story behind the word – how it has evolved over time and developed its current meaning. This can be coupled with visual representations to help further student's understanding. This might be an image that links to the meaning of the word (such as a yoke for subjugate) or visually separating the word to its component parts.

3   Examples

This stage is where scholars apply their understanding of a word by using it in different contexts to demonstrate accurate and meaningful use. However, this is also where misconceptions can surface if their understanding isn't fully secure. To address this, using an 'I Do-We Do-You Do' approach with mini whiteboards can be an effective strategy for checking comprehension. While it might be tempting to focus on selecting correct examples during whole-class activities, identifying and incorporating non-examples is equally valuable. Non-examples provide an excellent opportunity to uncover misconceptions, clarify misunderstandings, and reinforce accurate word usage.

Questions might include:

○ Which of these sentences uses subjugate correctly?
○ Remind me again, what does subjugate mean?
○ How do you know that you are using the word correctly?
○ Why do you think that is correct?

4   Synonyms

Comparing synonyms helps scholars recognise subtle differences in meaning and usage. For example, *subjugate* and *control* share similarities, but *subjugate* carries a more forceful, oppressive implication. Discussing these distinctions helps scholars apply words more accurately in context. By introducing synonyms within the Frayer Model, students learn more than one word at a time. This approach creates opportunities to extend their vocabulary and make links with other vocabulary.

Graphic organisers: Mind maps

Mind maps for essay planning and extended writing are probably something that you're already familiar with and use as part of your classroom practice. I'm including them in this section as they can also be incredibly beneficial in supporting scholars to think about how they create and track a character/theme/line of argument in order to develop a robust and cohesive thesis. Knowing how to establish and develop a 'golden thread' in writing begins in the planning phase. Obviously, scholars will not have the time, in high-stakes examinations, to create detailed writing plans; however, this does not mean they should not be planning in examination conditions. Instead, modelling the extended process to scholars (so that they understand how an expert learner approaches planning) and then moving them towards a skeleton structure will provide them with a framework to articulate their thinking logically and effectively.

Example mind map

How does Shakespeare present the **relationship** between Lady Macbeth and Macbeth in the play?

Thesis statement
- Initially presented as intimate/'equal'.
- Changed by witches; prediction to combative.
- Relationship begins to fracture after Duncan's murder – becomes increasingly isolated.

1. Intimate/colluding
- Act 1, Scene 5
  - 'my **dearest partner** in greatness'
  - 'I may pour **my spirits** in thine ear'
  - Treasonous letter (risk)
  - Patriarchy
  - 'Partners' but not equal

2. Combative/manipulative
- Act 1, Scene 7
  - 'Art thou **afeard**'
  - 'Who dares do more, is **none**'
  - 'dashed the brains out, had I so **sworn** as **you**'

3. Guilt-bound/protective
- Act 3, Scene 2

○ 'these terrible dreams | That shake **us** nightly'
○ 'full of **scorpions** is my mind'
○ '**Be innocent** of the knowledge, dearest **chuck**'

4. Isolated/fractured

- Act 5, Scene 5
  ○ 'She **should** have died **hereafter**'
  ○ 'There **would have** been a **time** for such a word'
  ○ 'signifying **nothing**'
  ○ Lady Macbeth dies alone
  ○ Switch positions
  ○ Macbeth focused on battle

Conclusion

- Shakespeare uses the relationship to demonstrate the of tyranny and guilt on even the strongest of partnerships.
- Like their souls, their relationship is cursed from the moment they carried out Duncan's murder (Table 9.1).

Table 9.1 Steps for a metacognitive mind map

Step	What?	Why?
1	Place a specific question/task in the centre.	A specific focus is more representative on an extended writing task. It also gives a focus point for scholars to refer to and ask themselves: am I answering the question?
2	Add four branches	Each branch will represent a key concept, which will be developed into an extended paragraphs when written up.
		Four concepts provide scholars with the opportunity to write in both breadth and depth within their response
3	Identify four main parts of the text, which best support a detailed response.	A chronological approach supports tracking throughout a text. It also lends itself to an effective method of demonstrating how a character/theme changes (or does not change) throughout the text and the catalysts to those changes.
	These need to be in chronological order and include both the beginning and the end of where a character/theme emerges.	
		With branches two and/or three, encourage scholars to think about parts of the text which are not as obvious (such as the scene where Lady Macbeth feints to distract attention from Macbeth) as it will offer a different perspective to other scholars' responses.
4	Select key vocabulary to summarise how the character is developed in each of the four sections. Students should monitor to ensure these also relate directly to the question they are answering.	The key vocabulary can be used to develop topic sentences. It also provides a focus for monitoring. Scholars should be asking themselves – do the quotations and examples I've chosen, link to the key words.

(Continued)

Table 9.1 Steps for a metacognitive mind map *(Continued)*

Step	What?	Why?
5	Select 2 quotations for each section that link to the question/key vocabulary.	These need to be "juicy" quotation (short and support a thoughtful response to the text).
6	Circle and annotate key vocabulary in quotations.	This helps students focus on the vocabulary they need to analyse effectively in their response.
7	Use key words from step 4 to create a thesis statement that can be used in the introduction.	This will establish a coherent argument and golden thread throughout the response.
8	Reflect on key words to create a conclusion that summarises the thread of the essay.	This supports an evaluative approach where students can comment on the extent a character theme has changed, what caused the changes and the impact of the changes throughout the text.

Adapting for examination planning

Once scholars understand the concept of mind mapping to track and structure their response to a text, the detail can be stripped away to establish a skeleton map that can be created quickly in examination conditions. In addition to giving scholars a coherent structure to their writing, it also supports how they manage cognitive load. Instead of trying to remember quotations/context/close reference to the text, they can recall and 'dump' this information in their plan and direct their attention on developing their plan.

Key word quizzing

Effective intellectual preparation should always consider the core disciplinary vocabulary scholars require to be able to: access the lesson materials; understand key concepts; communicate with precision, and prepare them for next steps in their learning. Curriculum planning should, therefore, take a planning backwards approach – considering the key word students need to know to access the lesson, the unit, the assessment, and the key stage terminal assessment. Key word knowledge also needs to be portable, so it can be taken from the lesson and used confidently and accurately in different contexts. This can be done by considering the vocabulary students need to know for GCSE texts and cascading them down to Years 7–9. For example, using a *Richard III* unit in Y9 to teach and secure some of the vocabulary they will need to access *Macbeth* in year 10.

Richard III portable vocabulary:

- Usurp
- Tyranny
- Duplicity
- Betrayal
- Conscience
- Paranoia
- Prophesy

- Nemesis
- Manipulation
- Machiavellian
- Integrity
- Loyalty
- Hubris
- Ambiguity
- Corruption

Essentially, it is not enough for students to be taught key words, they also need to be remembered in the long term! I have definitely been guilty of teaching students complex vocabulary (such as somnambulism and nihilism in *Macbeth*) and then never referring it again after the lesson. Like my teaching of these words, scholars recall of them faded when they did not encounter them again. Fortunately, we can avoid this by ensuring scholars have a secure understanding of the keyword when it is first taught and through repeated practice and recall.

Understanding can be secured by using methods, such as the Frayer Model in Figure 9.1, or explicit instruction where students learn simple definitions with examples and then non-examples.

Key vocabulary

Duplicity (noun): When someone lies or tricks others by pretending to be something they're not.
Duplicitous (adjective): Describing a person who lies or is dishonest on purpose.

Correct examples
- Richard III uses **duplicity** to trick people so he can become king.
- The boy was **duplicitous** and cheated in the quiz.

Incorrect examples
- Richard is **duplicity** because he wants to be king.
- My brother was **duplicitous** for forgetting my birthday.

To ensure vocabulary is secured in the long-term memory, they should have multiple, interleaved opportunities to recall and apply it accurately. This can be done by though simple recall activities, such as 'define hubris', or 'list two quotations that demonstrate Duncan's hubris' to more thoughtful application tasks, such as, 'Give three example of Mr Birling's hubris in *An Inspector Calls*' and 'How does Richard's hubris lead to his downfall'. Mini white boards are brilliant at maximising scholar participation and providing rapid, whole-class feedback, which can be followed up by targeted questioning.

Monitoring

Let us now turn our attention to ways to develop monitoring skills in our classroom.

Checklists

Checklists can be both a blessing and a curse! While I completely understand how giving scholars stabilisers, such as PEE (Point, Evidence, Explanation) can be a helpful starting point, too often this support is not faded out. Instead, checklists become further entrenched so that students become shackled by complex writing structures that must adhere to PETAL, PEZALAC, or SEELAC! Who hasn't been guilty of using AFOREST to teach persuasive writing? I'm afraid I have and it took me quite a while to burn those trees to the ground!

So where can checklists support monitoring effectively? Let me begin with the humble topic sentence. If scholars understand the three component parts of a topic sentence (it's accurate; it answers the question and it focuses on one idea/topic), it gives them a checklist to interrogate and monitor the accuracy of their writing. Furthermore they can then use these same three components to supporting with apt evidence. This does not mean you can only take one idea from the quotation, just that it should securely link to the topic sentence.

We can apply this same approach to supporting scholars to developing their analytical writing by using checklist question, rather than checklist structures. For an analytical response to a text this could include:

- Have I begun with an accurate topic sentence that outlines my position?
- Have I supported my topic sentence with a relevant, 'juicy' quotation?
- Have I embedded my quotation?
- Have I picked key vocabulary out of the quotation to analyse?
- Are there any other meaning of keywords that suggest alternative interpretations?
- Have I used tentative vocabulary?
- Have I referred to literary techniques?
- Have I used appositives to explore the effect of literary techniques, rather than identify them?
- Can I make any relevant links to context?
- Can I make any links to other parts of the text?
- What might be the writer's intention?
- Does this change the reader's/audience's perspective?
- Have I spelt the writer's name correctly and only referred to their surname?

I appreciate that is quite the list and I'm not suggesting that scholars work their way through the list for every paragraph. However, beginning with a simple checklist which is developed and then faded away so that students internalise it, may give them a more sophisticated set of options than a rigid PEZAL checklist.

Warning signs

Building a fruitful learning environment means creating a classroom where our scholars can make mistakes and, crucially, learn from them. One way we can support this is by leaning into mistakes and showing scholars the warning signs to look for as they work through a task. When we want our scholars to progress and work to a certain standard we can sometimes think the best way to do this is only by showing students perfect exemplars and unpicking the strengths. There is definitely value in this, especially when these exemplars are constructed via think alouds, where we show scholars how an expert learner approaches the task. However, we can also support our scholars by modelling deliberate mistakes and showing them the warning signs to look out for as they complete a task.

When planning, we can take one of two general approaches to developing warning signs: we can either anticipate misconceptions and mistake and pre-teach warning signs, or respond to misconceptions and mistakes by showing the warning signs to look out for next time. Whichever approach is taken (and it will probably be a combination on both) the key is to model the mistakes, explaining how and why they are mistakes and then create a warning signs checklist for students to use when monitoring their writing.

Let's assume that we have marked a piece of extended analysis for a mixed attainment Year 7 class and we have noticed the following errors in their academic writing.

- They are referring the author by their first name
- They are not embedding quotations accurately
- Using low level vocabulary

In this context, it can be really powerful to narrate the mistakes scholars have made in a modelled paragraph, while also questioning scholars and explaining why these are mistakes. For example:

> Charles presents Bill Sikes as a bad character. We know this because a quote in the book says he hurt Nancy because he "dragged her struggling and wrestling with him…" This shows that he was dragging her across a room and is not a very nice person.

Suggested questions and explanations

1 Why don't we call the writer by his first name?
   - It isn't academic
   - We don't know the writer personally
   - To show the reader that we are able to write academically
2 Is it an accurate topic sentence?
   - It is, but it isn't well written because it's basic and vague
3 What word can we use instead of bad?
   - Violent, brutal, merciless, and forceful

4 Why should we use a different word?
   ◦ To show precision – Sikes in bad in several different ways
   ◦ To show off your vocabulary
   ◦ To avoid repeating the same vague topic sentence later in our writing
5 What happens when we put a line through the line, '*We know this because a quote in the book says he hurt Nancy because he..?*'
   ◦ It supports embedding of quotations
   ◦ It saves time
   ◦ It removes a meaningless phrase that does not add anything to the response
   ◦ It shows the reader that we are able to write academically
6 How can we re-phrase our answer so we are embedding the quotation?
   ◦ 'Dickens presents Bill Sikes as a violent character with Nancy when he, dragged her struggling and wrestling with him. . .' OR
   ◦ 'Dickens presents Bill Sikes as a violent to Nancy, this is exemplified when he, dragged her struggling and wrestling with him. . .' OR
   ◦ 'Dickens presents Bill Sikes as a violent to Nancy, for example he, dragged her struggling and wrestling with him. . .'
7 What is/are the key word/words in the quotation that demonstrate Sikes' violence?
   ◦ 'dragged' and 'struggling'
8 Why isn't the last sentence analytical?
   ◦ We are narrating what happens in the quotation, rather than focusing on key words and their effects
   ◦ We are repeating words from the quotation without analysing them
   ◦ We are offering a simplistic view personal response of Sikes
9 How can we rewrite the final sentence to make it more analytical?
   ◦ 'This demonstrates that Sikes is not only pulling Nancy brutally across the room against her will, but also that he does not care that he is hurting her'. OR
   ◦ 'The act of pulling Nancy across the floor demonstrates his violent tendencies. This is made to seem especially shocking by Nancy's status as his girlfriend, whom he does not appear to care if he hurts, even though she loves him'. OR
   ◦ 'This suggests Sikes' behaves cruelly because he pulls her forcefully across the room and does not seem to care that he hurts her'.

I appreciate that there are quite a lot of questions there, for three analytical sentences, and I am not suggesting that they should all be used in one session. However, they do demonstrate the premise behind the questions – that narrating and then correcting mistakes can be just as powerful, if not more powerful, that just providing correct exemplar materials.

Once these mistakes have been unpicked, they can be codified in a warning signs checklist, to remind students of the mistakes they could make and how to avoid them. For the above example, these may include:

Charles presents Bill Sikes as a bad character. We know this because a quote in the book says he hurt Nancy because he "dragged her struggling and wrestling with him. . ." This shows that he was dragging her across a room and is not a very nice person.

As with all monitoring strategies, warning signs are designed to be used as scholars work through a task, so they can correct and change their approach where necessary. Ultimately, though we need our students to master these skills so they are both internalised and done automatically. It is at this point we can range the level of challenge, providing the 'Goldilocks' level of desirable difficulty required for them to progress (Sweller, 1994, 2011).

Evaluation

Finally, let us consider approaches that we can take to develop evaluative skills in our students.

Self/peer marking

Ultimately, we want all our scholars to be self-marking their work, both as they complete their work and once complete. We are not going to be there in a terminal, or independent assessment, stood over their shoulders, reminding them to include apt quotation or begin sentences with capital letters. Internalising checklists and knowing how to improve can be a powerful tool to help scholars evaluate and develop their responses. However, peer and self-marking can be problematic, if not managed carefully. If scholars are not clear of success criteria then they're in danger of guessing progress and/or giving inaccurate feedback. Providing student with a clear checklist, that they understand how to apply accurately, as shown in Table 9.2, can be an effective step in helping scholars know what and how to assess.

Table 9.2 Learning checklist

Accuracy check:	Yes/No
1 I have used an accurate topic sentence.	
2 I have embedded an apt quotation.	
3 I have used modal verbs to support tentative analysis.	
4 I have spelt Shakespeare correctly.	

Although checklists are useful, they are only as proficient as the scholar using them. Scholar proficiency can be increased incrementally by using techniques such as 'show tell', 'modelling', and 'prove it'.

Step 1

When scholars have completed the task, place one example under the visualiser and model to students how you prove they have met the requirements of the learning checklist (see Table 9.2). Highlighting an annotating the work is a useful way of getting scholars to justify feedback and makes it easier for you (and the scholar receiving the feedback) to see where they have met the criteria.

Step 2

Select a different scholar's work and place under visualiser. Ask student to read through the work then, on the count of three, mark (by holding up their fingers) how many elements of the learning checklist have been met. Questioning can also be used at this point to secure student understanding and address misconceptions. For example:

- Why have you given this scholar two out of three?
- How has this scholar has met checkpoint two?
- How could this student meet checkpoint one?
- What feedback would you give this student to improve?

Step 3

Once you are confident that scholars understand to apply the learning checklist accurately, they can independently apply it. As they become more proficient you can fade away this scaffolding as they internalise the success criteria and increase challenge by repeating the cycle with higher level criteria checklists.

In a nutshell, peer/self-marking really benefits from adhering to a *metacognitive* I Do – We Do–You Do structure and using very specific criteria that scholars can apply to their/ peers' work.

Reflection tasks

Reflection tasks help take scholar evaluation to the next level and form the final stage of the metacognitive cycle. In reflection tasks, scholars go beyond evaluating how successful they have been to considering what they need to keep doing and what to change in order to progress. WWW/EBI (What Went Well/Even Better If) style feedback can address this to an extent; however, this focuses on what students need to improve, rather than how to improve. I have seen so many scholar books where teachers have given ostensibly helpful feedback comments, such as 'analyse more' or 'spell accurately', without any suggestion of how to do this. This is problematic as it not only lacks specificity/breaks down the feedback (what feature of analytical writing exactly should the scholar focus on first?) but also assumes that scholars already know how to do this. I am pretty sure that if some scholars knew securely how to 'write more analytically' they would do just that!

Supporting reflection through teacher feedback

Targeted questions/checklists are a useful way of isolating specific aspects of the disciplinary or procedural knowledge you want to apply to their work and point them towards exactly what and how they need to do to improve. Consider the following four pieces of feedback and think about which is going to be more useful in supporting scholars to reflect on and improve their analytical writing.

a Write more analytically.
b Use tentative vocabulary to write more analytically.
c Include tentative vocabulary, by using modal verbs, to write more analytically.
d Include tentative vocabulary, by using modal verbs (such as this *could* suggest, this *may* infer), to write more analytically.

We can further support out scholars to reflect by ensuring they understand why, they need do something. In the above example, explaining that we use tentative vocabulary to:

- demonstrate to the reader that we are interpreting authorial intent and cannot definitely know if there is more than one interpretation
- show academic humility (we know we do not have the final answer)
- support probing of multiple meaning and ambiguities (*Dicken's use of 'dashed' may suggest that Sikes is in a hurry to murder Nancy, demonstrating his impulsive and rash behaviour. However, this verb also has connotations of violence, perhaps foreshadowing the brutal actions Sikes will take to end Nancy's life.*)

Of course, for this to be truly reflective, scholars need to take ownership of their performance, which can be supported by developing a reflection template, as shown in Table 9.3. As caveated at the start (and most of the way through) this chapter, using a think aloud as part of the I Do-We Do-You Do process can maximise impact and increase understanding of how to effectively reflect.

Table 9.3 Reflection template

What specifically do I need to improve?	Why specifically do I need to do this?	What can I due to improve next time I tackle a similar task?
Putting it into practice (class think aloud):		
Putting it into practice (independent work):		

In essence, embedding metacognition into English lessons empowers scholars to take control of their own learning. By encouraging them to plan, monitor, and evaluate their thinking, we help them become more independent, reflective, and resilient learners.

Whether they are analysing a literary text, crafting an argument, or developing their writing, metacognitive strategies support deeper understanding and improved outcomes. As teachers, fostering this awareness equips scholars not just for success in English, but for life beyond the classroom.

References

Clark, J. M., & Paivio, A. (1991). Dual coding theory and education. *Educational Psychology Review, 3*(3), 149–210.

Dowey, S. J. (2023). *Metacognition and Macbeth: Using lessons from cognitive science to teach Shakespeare in schools* (PhD thesis, University of York).

Gascoine, L., Tracey, L., Fairhurst, C., Robinson-Smith, L., Torgerson, D., Torgerson, C., & Bell, K. (2022). *ReflectED evaluation report*. Education Endowment Foundation.

Motteram, G., Choudry, S., Kalambouka, A., Hutcheson, G., & Barton, H. (2016). *ReflectED: Evaluation report and Executive summary*. Education Endowment Foundation.

Perry, T., Lea, R., Jørgensen, C. R., Cordingley, P., Shapiro, K., & Youdell, D. (2021). *Cognitive science in the classroom*. London: Education Endowment Foundation (EEF).

Quigley, A., Muijs, D., & Stringer, E. (2018). *Metacognition and self-regulated learning: Guidance report*. London: Education Endowment Foundation (EEF).

Sweller, J. (1994). Cognitive load theory, learning difficulty, and instructional design. *Learning and Instruction, 4*(4), 295–312.

Sweller, J. (2011). Cognitive load theory. *Psychology of Learning and Motivation, 55*, 37–76.

10

The humanities

Benjie Groom

Introduction

The application of metacognitive strategies to traditional humanities subjects, namely history, geography, and religious education, does not, at first, appear completely natural. With distinct pedagogies, the discussion surrounding each of these subjects' educational domains tends to be focused entirely on the substantive and disciplinary and less on broad practices such as metacognition. The highly contextual demands of many questions that pupils are asked and tasks that they are asked to complete in these lessons often force thoughts of the more general to one side.

However, plenty of metacognitive strategies exist alongside and underneath the demands of these subjects, often without teachers' and their pupils' knowledge. This chapter will aim to illuminate some of these and offer suggestions as to their natural places within the humanities. It will also suggest which strategies are particularly useful for pupils studying the humanities at GCSE level. At Key Stage 4, the repeatable demands of content delivery, note-taking, revision, and examination practice, all lend themselves to the use of the metacognitive strategies outlined below.

Planning

Here are some metacognitive strategies relating to planning.

Graphic organisers

The need to organise sequences of events in history, geography, and religious studies naturally lends itself to the use of flow maps of various types. In history, pupils are often required to write chronological narrative accounts. Having pupils approach this task by first using a flow map to plot out the key events in chronological order can support the quality of their responses. For example, when teaching pupils about the key events in USA-USSR relations during the period 1943–1949, a flow map that outlines the various important events in chronological order will support pupils in recalling this period accurately and with a clear understanding of how the events link together. Similarly, in geography, pupils might need to describe the stages of a natural disaster and the human response to it. Once more, a flow map will help pupils ensure their description is precise, well-ordered, and accurate.

In the humanities, pupils often need to recall the reasons for a particular event or development. In history, pupils regularly need to demonstrate knowledge of how different factors led to a particular outcome or result. Here, a fishbone diagram can be used with pupils to help them reflect on how different events played a causal role at different times or the way in which different events can be grouped according to their factors. Pupils often need to categorise causes in the humanities, and fishbone diagrams are perfect for this. You might lead pupils in reading a piece of text that describes a sequence of events and have them construct their own fishbone diagram. In doing so they will identify different factors, assign them to particular groups and therefore think more deeply about why something has occurred compared with a more superficial timeline or flowchart. In geography, for example, you might ask pupils to organise the primary and secondary impacts of the 2021 Haiti earthquake into social, economic, and environmental sections using this sort of diagram.

A common theme of the humanities subjects is the requirement for pupils to learn and retain a large amount of knowledge about particular events, concepts, case studies, developments, or events. In national examinations these are often referred to briefly in questions, and pupils can easily respond with only superficial knowledge related to whatever area they are being examined on. To avoid this, the regular use of brace maps can be very fruitful. For example, in religious education, pupils can be supported to answer questions about the Buddhist concept of Bhavachakra (the Wheel of Life). Encouraging students to note down the sum of their knowledge related to this concept, using a brace map, allows them to reflect firstly on what they do know and secondly on how different aspects of their knowledge are connected. This will allow them to answer questions about this idea with much greater detail and clarity and help them to include the knowledge that is most relevant to whatever question has been posed.

Problem-solving grids

Across the humanities, and especially in national examinations for these subjects, pupils are often required to answer the same sorts of questions, or to complete tasks that are a repetition of those they have completed before. For example, in history pupils are often required to analyse and evaluate the usefulness of a historical source. In religious studies, pupils often need to evaluate statements and, referring to religious teachings, give reasoned arguments that support and oppose it, coming to a justified conclusion. In geography, pupils are often required to evaluate the methods used to manage a particular ecological problem or natural hazard.

Across all of these examples, the use of planning grids can be transformative in helping pupils (especially those lacking confidence) structure better answers. Given the nature of content-heavy GCSE courses, examination practice is often spaced out across the curriculum, meaning that pupils may only encounter the same question types intermittently. Planning grids are incredibly useful to ameliorate this problem. By having pupils fully comprehend the task they are faced with, connect it to other or similar examples and then reflect on the strategies they might deploy in completing the task or question, we give them a much greater chance of success than merely setting a task or examination question.

The key to this approach lies in the full utilisation of well-prepared grids that provide pupils with all the stimulus questions that they need to comprehend, connect, strategise and evaluate. You might consider providing completed models during the first time using these grids to show pupils what a good one looks like and why they are so useful. Gradually, over time, these models can be removed and the number of stimulus questions removed in order to encourage automaticity in your students, in the hope that they can (maybe mentally) apply the thinking that underlies these grids when faced with unseen questions in exams.

Exam question analysis

The levels of response criteria used to mark humanities questions in national examinations mean that developing a working knowledge of what good exam question answers look like through exam question analysis is a highly valuable metacognitive strategy to use with pupils across these subjects.

You may wish to operate a faded approach to this strategy in order to develop pupils' metacognitive skills in this area. For example, in history, when working with pupils to develop knowledge of effective source evaluation, teachers may wish to guide pupils through the features of a good answer, highlighting and annotating the use of contextual knowledge, discussion of content and provenance, and the clarity of the judgements that are presented. This can be projected on a traditional whiteboard or through the use of a visualiser, with pupils noting down the teacher's analysis on their own copies. The next time this question type is encountered, the teacher may wish to remove some of this scaffolding, reminding pupils of the key features to look out for while they work in pairs or individually to find these in the model response. Eventually, model answers can be used merely as an aide-memoir for pupils to respond to similar questions and ultimately be withdrawn completely so that they can create their own high-quality responses informed by their metacognitive work on what makes a good answer in this domain.

The same approach can be applied to longer exam questions in both religious education and geography in a very similar manner.

Monitoring

Let us now consider metacognitive strategies relating to monitoring.

Key questions

The vast majority of tasks or questions that pupils face in the humanities subjects are fairly significant in terms of the stress they place on cognitive load. Take, for example, examination questions such as:

- 'Belief in Jesus is all that Christians need to be saved from sin.' Evaluate this statement

or

- In the period 1800–present, the main reason for improvement in dealing with infectious diseases was the role of government. How far do you agree?

Both are examples of substantial questions that require pupils to balance large amounts of contextual and domain-specific knowledge when forming an answer. They need to remember and apply their understanding of the question's contextual and conceptual demands, which can be very taxing, leaving many unable to construct a rigorous or well-structured answer. The use of key questions to break down a task or question like these can be a worthwhile metacognitive approach to help pupils with this issue.

With the first example, teachers may wish to break down the question into various sub-questions such as:

- What are the Christian teachings about sin and being saved from sin?
- Do Christians believe that belief in Jesus is one way to be saved from sin?
- Is this the only Christian belief about how Christians can be saved from sin?
- Are there any non-religious teachings or views about how people can be saved from sin?
- What are the arguments in favour of this statement?
- What are the arguments against this statement?
- Overall, which of these arguments do you find most compelling?

By doing so, the task becomes much more manageable and allows pupils to use more of their knowledge to respond to the question. Some of these sub-questions will be specific to the task itself, but others can be generic, applying to questions with the same structure or mark scheme. Here, having pupils memorise these generic questions can be very useful as it will ensure that they cover specific aspects of a question's mark scheme that they might otherwise miss out, for example, evaluation.

As with many other strategies, it is best to introduce this first as a teacher-led approach before 'fading out' teacher support until pupils can complete this sort of thinking with minimal prompting.

Content checklists

In the humanities, where pupils are regularly required to explain or make judgements about particular statements, events, or developments, they are often able to replicate pre-rehearsed writing structures in response to questions or tasks they are faced with. They are also able to include a sufficient level of contextual knowledge to support the analysis or evaluation they have presented. Where pupils sometimes fall down, however, is in their coverage of a range of contextual information in their responses.

The vast majority of mark schemes for longer examination questions in the humanities subjects require both breadth and depth of knowledge or a range of the same.

The 'content checklist' can be very valuable for coaching pupils to ensure they include as much appropriate knowledge as possible in their answers.

Take, for example, the examination question:

- Explain how the Nazis used propaganda to control the German people.

A content checklist for this question would be as follows:

- The NSDAP censored newspaper content, sometimes even on Hitler or Goebbels' personal orders.
- The NSDAP organised annual mass rallies at a special stadium in Nuremberg.
- The NSDAP produced antisemitic cartoons, films, posters, and literature.
- The NSDAP controlled radio broadcasts and made mass radio ownership possible through the production of cheap radio sets with short-wave frequencies that would not pick up foreign broadcasts.
- The NSDAP organised mass book burnings.

A strong answer to the question would mention all of these examples, explaining how each contributed to how the Nazi Party used propaganda to control the German people. By asking pupils to write a content checklist like this before answering the question, teachers can help them include far more specific contextual information in their answers than they might otherwise have.

This strategy can be modelled for pupils and conducted as a whole-class activity (it can be beneficial to challenge pupils to 'find one more thing' to create as long a checklist as possible) completed in pairs or eventually as an individual activity in response to unseen questions. The goal is to make this metacognitive practice a key one that pupils deploy when faced with questions requiring a broad exemplification of their knowledge of a particular topic or subject.

Task success criteria

As we have discussed elsewhere, the humanities subjects often require pupils to produce lengthy responses to questions. Where national examinations are concerned, these responses require a number of interrelated features to be deemed successful. Furthermore, as pupils progress through these questions, they often become more challenging, requiring pupils to repeat some skills while introducing new ones.

For example, in GCSE RE, pupils might be asked to outline some Buddhist teachings about Buddha-nature, explain reasons why *metta* is important for Buddhists, explain reasons why the founding of the Sangha is important to Buddhists (referring to a source of wisdom and authority) and finally evaluate the statement: "It is possible to end suffering", considering arguments for and against while referring to Buddhist teachings and reaching a justified conclusion.

Task comprehension is critical, therefore, for pupils to respond in the most effective way possible to a variety of different questions. Here, task success criteria can be incredibly helpful. In essence this is a list of all of the factors that are required in a response or answer. In the case of GCSE questions, this can be developed from appropriate mark-schemes and in the case of other tasks, whatever marking rubric that is being used can be adapted to produce these criteria.

Taking the example question above where pupils are required to explain reasons why the founding of the Sangha is important to Buddhists, a set of task success criteria might look like the following:

- State two reasons why Sangha is important to Buddhists.
- Explain each reason further with at least another sentence to develop it.
- For at least one of your reasons, refer to a source of Buddhist wisdom or authority.

Armed with such a set of task success criteria for the various questions they encounter, pupils will be well prepared to respond in the correct manner.

As with other metacognitive techniques such as content checklists or key questions, this strategy can be implemented by teachers first before 'fading out' support to eventually have the pupils themselves produce these task success criteria. Teachers might like to involve a mid-way point in this gradual withdrawal of support whereby they act as a facilitator for a class or group to produce the criteria collectively, intervening only where necessary.

Evaluation

This section looks at metacognitive strategies for evaluation.

Self/peer marking

As we have seen so far across this chapter, the humanities subjects often require pupils to construct developed responses to particular questions. These sorts of responses are usually complex and require pupils to juggle a variety of knowledge, literacy, and examination technique challenges. While we as teachers do our best to convey the intricacies of what is needed through our teaching, it can also be useful for pupils to evaluate the degree to which they, or their peers, have met these requirements. The foundational principle for this metacognitive technique is that feedback serves many purposes. Here, the purpose is to improve the pupil, rather than their responses. Seeing as it is impossible for us to predict the specific questions that pupils might face in their examinations, this strategy serves to reinforce pupils' thinking about how to answer these questions and catch misconceptions that may arise.

This technique works best when pupils know in advance that their responses will be self or peer assessed, rather than by their teacher. This, along with explaining to pupils that they will not receive a summative grade or mark for the piece of work that is being assessed, allows the focus of the activity to be placed firmly on formative feedback.

The use of self or peer marking relies on the quality of the assessment materials provided to pupils and the guidance that teachers can give to pupils. Teachers should think carefully about the resources they give to pupils from which they will be self or peer assessing. Some success can come from using examination mark schemes, but these are often riddled with technical jargon or difficult to decipher the language. Instead, teachers might consider taking these mark schemes and rewriting them in 'pupil-friendly' styles or with changed terminology. This of course varies from question to question and subject to subject, but an example can be found below:

Let us say that a geography mark scheme for this question "'Urban change in the UK has created more economic opportunities than social opportunities.' Evaluate this statement. Use a UK city you have studied" requires pupils to "demonstrate thorough application of knowledge and understanding to make a thorough evaluation of the relative merit of social/economic opportunities in a UK city". This could well be impenetrable to some pupils, so for this strand of the mark scheme, teachers could provide the more pupil-friendly:

"1. Your knowledge of social and economic opportunities in a UK city is used to answer the question. You do not give knowledge just for the sake of it.

2. You explain whether more social or economic opportunities have been created by urban change in a UK city. You do not just count the number of opportunities, but you explain why some of these opportunities are more important than others e.g., they affect more people or are longer lasting."

This approach serves two functions. First, it makes it much easier for pupils to self- or peer-assess their work. Second, it helps pupils improve their understanding of what is required of them, elucidating what can be a complicated set of success criteria.

One final consideration for self or peer marking is the faded way in which teachers might seek to support pupils in its use. This strategy is most effective when teachers support pupils in the early attempts before gradually fading this support out, eventually leaving pupils to self or peer mark with limited teacher direction. This can be accomplished by modelling the marking of a piece of work using the same resources given to pupils for the first couple of attempts (either using a visualiser or on an interactive or traditional whiteboard) before moving to shared marking, with suggestions from the class, and finally self or peer marking without direct teacher input. When pupils begin to feel comfortable with this practice, the teacher's attention can then turn to circulation in order to check on pupils' attempts and to correct and misconceptions that arise during the process.

Learning diaries

Learning diaries give students the opportunity to record various facets of their learning over a period of time, helping them to develop their metacognitive toolset and make them more reflective learners.

It is a technique that works particularly well in the humanities subjects due to their use of enquiry. Across history, geography, and religious education, units of learning are often sequenced in the form of enquiries focused around a central question. For example, in RE pupils might spend several lessons answering the question, 'What can census data tell us about modern Anglicanism?', in geography pupils might investigate a question like, 'Why do people live near natural hazards?' and in history they might tackle, 'How did religious change affect people in Tudor England?'. In answering all of these questions, pupils undertake a substantive and disciplinary journey where they end up knowing and understanding more in terms of skills and knowledge.

During these enquiries, the central question is often returned to at various points so that pupils can reflect on how their answer to the question changes over time based on new information and teaching. These interruptions mark the perfect point for pupils to reflect not just on the central question, but on their learning as well, particularly their identified areas of strength and the areas that they need to improve and revise.

For example, having learnt about the impact of Henry VIII and Edward VI's reforms to the Church, pupils might take stock to reflect on the impact this had on ordinary people in England. At the same time you could also ask them to reflect on the reading and note-taking strategies they have used, the time they have taken to prepare for knowledge quizzes, their performance in low-stakes quizzing, and formative assessment opportunities or the amount of work outside of the classroom they have completed to support their learning.

Furthermore, this diary could be completed with other tasks identified above, such as self-assessment or by including 'exit ticket' style tasks that require pupils to reflect on that lesson's learning. In addition, you might ask pupils to reflect on which metacognitive strategies pupils have used so far in the unit, and how effective they have found these.

Self-motivation is hopefully a helpful product of the use of these learning diaries, whereby students can see their progress across either a unit or across a longer span of time if they were to compare one learning diary to that of another. Here, you might use reflection time at the beginning or end of a unit to instruct pupils to compare their learning diaries from different units so that they can focus on a particular metacognitive skill in the upcoming learning.

Exam wrappers

Examination papers in the humanities subjects, especially at GCSE level, often contain a variety of question styles and lengths. Pupils are required to juggle various things at once. They need to recall and apply multiple answer formats, keep an eye on their timing and of course recall the necessary contextual knowledge needed to answer each question.

Accordingly, their attainment in a summative assessment that has an examination style format depends on their ability to be consistent across the subject's skills, knowledge, and understanding of exam technique. As teachers we want to ensure that our feedback for assessments like these will result in a meaningful change in our pupils. Exam wrappers are an effective tool to accomplish this, and have the added bonus of helping pupils to form metacognitive habits.

Exam wrappers can take many formats but will record the questions from an assessment, the marks on offer and a range of reflective tasks. They are particularly effective for the humanities subjects as they allow feedback to be distilled in one place so that teacher and pupil alike can look for patterns or trends in performance.

Exam wrappers can be used flexibly depending on your requirements. For example, if you want your pupils to reflect on why they lost marks, it can be useful to produce an exam wrapper that records the reasons why pupils got the marks they did. This can then be used as a basis for reflection regarding the common reasons for them doing so. Alternatively, where pupils are more familiar with the requirements of the exam or the questions they faced, you may wish to provide less feedback at this level, and the exam wrapper could contain some self-assessment rubrics that pupils need to use to identify exactly where and how they lost the marks they did.

As well as helping pupils to identify where they went wrong, or what they did well, in particular questions, exam wrappers can be used in an even more metacognitively active manner, albeit in a retrospective fashion. Directed questions can be included to prompt pupils to reflect on both their preparation for the assessment and the exam techniques they utilised. For example, you might ask some of the following questions for pupils to answer.

Preparation reflection

- How long did you spend preparing for this assessment?
- Which of the following preparation techniques did you use?
  - Mind-mapping
  - Re-writing notes
  - Self-quizzing
  - Flash cards
  - Answering practice questions
  - Other...
- Where and when did you undertake your preparation for this assessment?
- Did any topics come up that you did not feel adequately prepared for?
- If so, why?

Exam technique reflection

- Did you have enough time to complete the assessment?
- If not, which question(s) did you not finish?
- Did you attempt the questions in the paper order, or a different one? Why?

- How much did you write for shorter, lower mark questions compared with longer, higher mark questions?
- Did you plan your responses to the longer questions? If so, why not? What form did these plans take? Did you follow these plans when writing?

These self-reflection questions can have a really powerful metacognitive effect, especially when combined with some of the other techniques discussed in this chapter. Your exam wrappers could make reference to content checklists or task success criteria to provide continuity between the various metacognitive strategies that you provide your pupils with.

11

Music and performing arts

Kirsten Johnson

Introduction

The performing arts department has a habit of being 'othered' from the rest of the school; either by departments themselves ('we are a practical subject and therefore strategy x and non-negotiable y isn't applicable to us') or by the way in which the subjects are perceived by others, such as the long-held belief that artistic subjects are inherently non-academic. I would argue that the performing arts are neither totally 'practical subjects' nor 'non-academic'. As with any skill, there is a large amount of theoretical and procedural knowledge that must be applied to a physical performance and realisation of the skill in question.

The theory of metacognition is therefore well applied to music and performing arts. students who have a deep understanding of what they know, what they don't know, and how this must be utilised in the context of their chosen performing arts strand, are far more able to improve their output. In this chapter I will use the term 'performing arts' to refer to the study of music, drama, technical production arts, dance and musical theatre in general. Where necessary, I will specify the particular branch of study, as it relates to the metacognitive strategy under discussion.

Planning

Here are some metacognitive strategies relating to planning.

Graphic organisers

Graphic organisers are a great way for students to visualise what they already know, and to work through their thought process in order to synthesise their knowledge for the task at hand; be it a retrieval task in the classroom, a musical performance or the completion of an exam question at the end of the year.

In a study of SEND students, Dexter et al. (2011) found that "across several conditions, settings, and features, the use of graphic organisers was associated with increases in vocabulary knowledge, comprehension, and inferential knowledge." We know that quality-first teaching is appropriate for all students and so graphic organisers are a very accessible form of scaffolding, as the teacher can progress from using pre-printed organiser templates with headings, to blank templates, to ones which are fully student-created.

Flow maps are particularly appropriate for use in the drama classroom. This method of drawing out a sequence of events can be used to map out a story arc or character development over the course of the set text, allowing students to demonstrate their knowledge of the key transformation points in the story. This then allows them to map out, for instance, differences in costume, lighting or physicality appropriate to the character at these differing points. This knowledge is crucial to their understanding of the dramatic conventions utilised by both the playwright and the actor during performance. This knowledge and understanding is then often demonstrated in the answering of an exam question, along the lines of *"Read the given extract. Design a costume to be worn by Character X. Describe and explain your choices with reference to both the specific scene and the wider story."* Students therefore must be confident in their knowledge of the play as a whole, the character development throughout the play, the placing of the given scene within the play, the time period of the play as whole, the fashions of this time period, and, the use of costume to convey character.

Exam question analysis

Love them or hate them, exam questions are designed to test both students' knowledge of the subject and their understanding of how key concepts are utilised in given examples. In GCSE Music, for example, students are presented with aural examples of either known or unknown musical pieces. In either case, the study of prior exam questions will support students in evaluating their current subject knowledge, identifying knowledge gaps and deciphering *what* the question is asking of them.

The ability to differentiate between *identify, state, describe, explain,* and *suggest* is a key skill for students. Guiding students through these definitions can be undertaken during class time, supported by number of short example questions. Once this has been undertaken over a series of lessons, students can then be given exam command words to define as part of a retrieval or plenary activity. Exam questions completed as part of classwork or homework are invaluable tools for discovering where gaps in knowledge exist.

Giving students their marked questions back to review is a great way to support their metacognitive development. Once they have their question paper in front of them, they can annotate it.

- Command word – did they read and action it correctly?
- Question content – did they interpret it correctly?
- Answer – was the content correct? Have they included information not asked for, simply because they know that information?

- Answer – was it a full answer, written in the correct format (a list, full sentences, essay style etc)?

This analysis can be undertaken in the style of a flow chart, as detailed in the above strategy, with remedial steps taken at each stage where an error is identified by the student. This flow chart, or a blank version, can then also be used to plan an answer to the same style of question in the future.

Knowledge organisers

Knowledge organisers are something that have gained a lot of popularity in the last decade or so, and for good reason. From a planning standpoint, creating knowledge organisers as a teacher or leader require a complete audit of the syllabus being covered which is a fantastic way to ensure that you aren't strayed too far away from the required content, simply because you have been teaching it for a long time.

Knowledge organisers are a really flexible document too – you can create an overview of the whole topic on a page, with additional organisers used to provide more granular detail of key areas.

In music, organisers can give an overview of musical eras and their key features, with additional organisers for key musical elements such as tempo, timbre, and structure.

Students can use teacher-created overview documents to create their own knowledge organisers, for example, utilising a given organiser on the music eras, timbre, and structure to create an organiser detailing the development of the Concerto through history.

An accurate Concerto knowledge organiser can then feed into exam question practice where students may be asked to listen to an aural extract and:

A   Identify the instrumentation
B   Describe the structure
C   Suggest the time period the extract is taken from
D   Explain their reasoning for their answer to C

In the above example, students would need to:

- Know the names of the instruments of the orchestra
- Know what the instruments sound like
- Know the names of common musical structures
- Categorise those structures as orchestral, solo instrumental, or vocal
- Define those structures
- Identify the structure when they hear it
- Know the key features of multiple musical eras: baroque, classical, romantic, 20th Century
- Articulate the era-specific features heard in the example which allowed them to narrow down their answer to C) (for example, the use of harpsichord being suggestive of music written in the baroque era).

Monitoring

The following strategies are concerned with monitoring.

Key questions

GCSE drama question structures vary between exam boards however all boards have the requirement for an extended answer, essay-style question.

In order to answer such questions fully, students can be encouraged to break the question down into smaller, sub-questions and answer these in turn, building up an answer to the original question.

For example:

- You are performing the role of Romeo
- Focus on the final third of the following extract, beginning with the line 'For fear of that I still will stay with thee'.
- Explain how you might use physical acting skills and the performance space to portray Romeo's grief to the audience.

> From Romeo and Juliet, Act 5, Scene 3:
> [Romeo opens the tomb to reveal Juliet inside]
> A grave? O no, a lantern, slaughtered youth,
> For here lies Juliet, and her beauty makes.
> This vault a feasting presence full of light.
> Death, lie thou there, by a dead man interred.
> [Lays PARIS in the tomb]
> How oft when men are at the point of death.
> Have they been merry! Which their keepers call.
> A lightning before death! O, how may I.
> Call this a lightning? O my love, my wife!
> Death that hath sucked the honey of thy breath,
> Hath had no power yet upon thy beauty.
> Thou art not conquered. Beauty's ensign yet.
> Is crimson in thy lips and in thy cheeks,
> And death's pale flag is not advanced there.
> Tybalt, liest thou there in thy bloody sheet?
> O, what more favour can I do to thee
> Than with that hand that cut thy youth in twain.
> To sunder his that was thine enemy?
> Forgive me, cousin. Ah, dear Juliet,
> Why art thou yet so fair? Shall I believe.
> That unsubstantial death is amorous;
> And that the lean abhorred monster keeps.
> Thee here in dark to be his paramour?
> For fear of that I still will stay with thee,

And never from this palace of dim night.

Depart again. Here, here will I remain.

With worms that are thy chambermaids. O, here.

Will I set up my everlasting rest,

And shake the yoke of inauspicious stars.

From this world-wearied flesh. Eyes, look your last.

Arms, take your last embrace! And, lips, O you.

The doors of breath, seal with a righteous kiss.

A dateless bargain to engrossing death.

[Kisses JULIET, takes out the poison]

Come, bitter conduct, come, unsavoury guide.

Thou desperate pilot, now at once run on.

The dashing rocks thy sea-sick weary bark.

Here's to my love! [Drinks the poison] O true apothecary!

Thy drugs are quick. Thus with a kiss I die.

[ROMEO Dies]

In order to answer the above question, students could break it down into the following sub-questions (Table 11.1).

Table 11.1   Breaking an exam question into sub-questions

a) *Who is Romeo?*	Romeo is a young man living in Verona, Italy. His family (the Montagues) are locked in a bitter feud with the Capulet family.
b) *What is his relationship to the others mentioned in the extract?*	Juliet is a young woman, younger than Romeo, who is a member of the Capulet family. She and Romeo meet, fall in love and marry within the space of days. Romeo is visiting Juliet's tomb where her body lies. He believes she is dead.
c) *What is his age in this extract?*	Romeo is around 16 years old.
d) *What characteristics does person of this age possess?*	Adolescent boys can experience a range of emotions, feeling each of them very strongly. Throughout the play we see many different sides to Romeo's personality – he is impulsive (initially he is madly in love with Rosaline but once he meets Juliet, he marries her almost immediately), he is quick to anger (killing Tybalt in revenge for Mercutio's death) and he drowns in grief from Juliet's death, taking his own life at her tomb.
e) *What is his socio-economic background?*	Romeo is from a very wealthy, privileged background.
f) *How is this conveyed to the audience in the play as a whole?*	Throughout the play we see Romeo acting with impunity, seemingly unconcerned with the consequences of his actions. He uses his connections in society to marry Juliet quickly and in secret. He takes revenge on Tybalt, killing him in retaliation for Mercutio's death.

(Continued)

Table 11.1 Breaking an exam question into sub-questions *(Continued)*

g) List the main acting skills you have studied	Physical acting skills include: • Eye contact • Body language • Facial expressions • Use of space • Use of levels • Movement/gait • Gesture • Pace
h) Link these acting skills to the characteristics you have listed above to Romeo's grief in the extract.	Romeo is used to getting his own way – he is wealthy, popular, and arrogant. Juliet's "death" creates a situation where he is no longer in control and he is unable to fix the situation he finds himself in. Rather than carrying on with his life without Juliet in exile, facing the consequences of Tybalt's murder, he chooses to end his own life. It is the actor's choice whether to portray his grief as being purely for the loss of Juliet, grief for the loss of control and status he once had, or a combination of the two.

Content checklists

Content checklists can be used independently, or in conjunction with the key questions technique above.

In my example, I have included a content checklist (Table 11.2) in my answer to sub-question g).

Table 11.2 An example of a content checklist

Physical acting skills include:
☐ Eye contact
☐ Body language
☐ Facial expressions
☐ Use of space
☐ Use of levels
☐ Movement/gait
☐ Gesture
☐ Pace

In GCSE music, students may find it helpful to list the elements of music (see Table 11.3) to help them answer an open-ended question.

(d) Describe how the solo instrument and the orchestra work together in this extract. [2]

Table 11.3 Elements of music content checklist

Elements of music	Metre and rhythm
☐ **Melody**	☐ **Metre and rhythm**
○ Ornamentation	○ Simple time
○ Conjunct movement	○ Compound time
○ Disjunct movement	○ Irregular time
○ Arpeggios	○ Changes of time signature
☐ **Harmony and Tonality**	○ Dotted rhythms
○ Major	○ Triplets
○ Minor	○ Cross rhythms
○ Modulation	○ Polyrhythms
○ Primary chords	☐ **Instrumentation**
○ Secondary chords	○ Instruments used
☐ **Texture**	○ Changes in the instruments used
○ Monophony	☐ **Dynamics**
○ Homophony	○ Dynamics used by each instrument/family
○ Heterophony	○ Changes in dynamics (sudden vs gradual)
○ Polyphony	○ Crescendo
○ Fugue	○ Diminuendo
○ Counterpoint	○ Sforzando
☐ **Structure**	○ Subito piano
○ AB	○ Contrasts in dynamics
○ ABA	☐ **Timbre**
○ ABACA	○ Legato
○ Strophic	○ Staccato
○ Verse and Chorus	○ Muted
○ Through-composed	○ Flutter tonguing
☐ **Tempo**	○ Amplified
○ Adagio	○ Distortion
○ Andante	
○ Allegro	
○ Vivace	
○ Ritardando	
○ Rallentando	
○ Accelerando	

The information contained in these checklists can be taken from knowledge organisers. The more the knowledge organisers are used for revision and classwork, the more
automated the process of listing the content checklists becomes. In an exam situation,
listing the headings should be sufficient to keep students on-track and including the
relevant details however in a classroom or homework situation, student may wish to add
further detail while they scaffold their answers.

Warning signs

Warning signs is a technique wherein students review their work as they are completing
it, to ensure that they are not veering off-track. Some exam questions will be broader in
nature and allow students some leeway in their answer while others will be explicit and

proscriptive in their wording. For example, in the below question students are directed towards specific elements of music in their answer. Any reference to additional elements of music, even if they are accurate, will not be rewarded in the mark scheme.

Question: This is the theme tune from the video game "Intergalactic Space Warriors". Write a paragraph, using sentences, explaining how the music conveys the scene of a battle in outer space. **You should refer only to instruments, rhythm and texture** *in your answer.*

Warning signs encourage students to stop at the end of each sentence or paragraph and check their work.

Are they answering the question that has been asked, or are they answering the question they know the answer to?

At the end of each section of their answer students go back and read the questions again and ask themselves:

- Did the question explicitly request specific information/themes in my answer?
- Have I included this yet?
- What have I not yet covered in my answer?
- Have I mentioned something not explicitly asked for?

This allows students the opportunity to self-edit as they write, learning how to focus their answers and develop skills to best utilise their time in exam situations. While all exams have a finite time limit, in some subjects students will be able to work through the exam paper at their own pace (for example, drama) however in a music exam which utilises timed audio excerpts students must answer questions at the pace of the audio tracks and as such may not be able to go back to a questions later and revise their answers. Being able to identify warning signs within their answers as they write is therefore particularly useful within the music classroom.

Evaluation

The next set of strategies concern evaluation.

Self/peer marking

The teacher marking burden is something which is often discussed in staffrooms and social media. By encouraging students to self and peer mark their work, we are not only reducing the marking burden for ourselves but supporting students to think critically about their own work.

Producing detailed marking criteria when devising an assessment or consolidation task not only ensures that the task functions appropriately but also reduces the need for onerous marking once completed.

Exam-board criteria are often vague and subjective, and therefore not appropriate for students.

Providing students with a breakdown of what each section of the marking criteria means in practice, preferably in conjunction with a high-quality exemplar, allows them to successfully analyse what has been successful in their own work, along with identifying which features they have not used, thus allowing them to identify their own next steps for improvement.

When marking exam coursework, we as teachers can keep a record of success utilising the exam board criteria but provide students with a list of suggested ways to implement these criteria. In this example (Table 11.4), we take a specific marking band broken down by the elements of music, giving students a more useable guide for reflection and improvement.

Table 11.4 An example of a music composition mark scheme broken down into individual elements

MELODY	Well-balanced four-bar phrases in theme	☑
MELODY	Range of techniques to develop the melody	☐
MELODY	Melody in different instruments at different times	☐
MELODY	Counter melody	☑
MELODY	Based variations on the theme – all variations can be traced back to the theme	☐
RHYTHM	Range of techniques to change the rhythm	☐
RHYTHM	Varied rhythms	☐
RHYTHM	No endless repetitive passages using the same rhythms	☐
HARMONY	Primary chords (I, IV, V)	☑
HARMONY	Secondary chords (ii, iii, vi, vii)	☐
	Number of features present in composition	3
	GCSE Criteria marks (out of 30)	8

Learning diaries

Learning diaries (see Tables 11.5 and 11.6) are an excellent resource for both music and drama students and are indeed required for some exam boards.

Introducing learning diaries to students in Key Stage 3 may take some time to embed but will pay dividends at GCSE as students will have developed the necessary self-reflection skills over time, and it will have become second nature to them to reflect on their performance.

Including a list of helpful strategies within the learning diary will support students to reflect on their journey of improvement.

Effective music practice strategies
- Identify the key of the piece you are learning
- Practice the scale and arpeggio of this key
- Choose a slow tempo
- Play small sections (four bars) at a time

- Connect these small sections by playing the end of Section A and the start of Section B
- Play the larger, connected sections
- Record your practice session – look at your technique and posture, listen to the rhythms you are playing

Examples of learning diary strategies.

Music and drama students must develop skills as well as knowledge. They may be required to demonstrate, as part of coursework or simply as a developmental task, that they have identified and improved.

- Their personal management skills,
- The ability to apply music performance skills in rehearsal,
- The ability to identify and describe both strengths and weaknesses in their own performance and rehearsals,

The ability to select and apply appropriate rehearsal techniques.

Table 11.5 An example of a learning diary strategy

Skills review: What have you learnt/ re-capped in this lesson?	Target setting: What do you need to practise before next lesson?
Techniques in performance	**Techniques in performance**
• Accuracy of notes	• Accuracy of notes
• Rhythm and timing	• Rhythm and timing
• Expression and dynamics	• Expression and dynamics
• Phrasing	• Phrasing
Techniques in rehearsal	**Techniques in rehearsal**
• Learning Repertoire	• Learning Repertoire
• Technical exercises (e.g., scales, arpeggios, paradiddles)	• Technical exercises (e.g., scales, arpeggios, and paradiddles)
Interpretation in performance	**Interpretation in performance**
• Emphasis of style	• Emphasis of style
• Reproduction of style	• Reproduction of style
• Awareness of accompaniment (backing track if used)	• Awareness of accompaniment (backing track if used)
• Physical expression	• Physical expression
• Communication	• Communication
• Confidence	• Confidence
• Stage presence	• Stage presence
• Interaction with audience	• Interaction with audience
• Musicality	• Musicality

Work Ethic: How would you say your **attitude** was this lesson?

Table 11.6 A further example of a learning diary strategy

	1 (Poor)	2 (Requires Improvement)	3 (Average)	4 (Good)	5 (Excellent)
Punctuality					
Organisation					
Behaviour					
Commitment					
Focus and Effort					
Technical Skills					
Interpretation/ Performance					
Overall Progress					

Good, better, and best answers

Students can often find open-ended, essay style questions overwhelming. There are a number of ways to build up their resilience towards answering these questions such as using knowledge organisers to support an open-book approach, using content checklists to scaffold an answer or using 'good, better, best' examples as part of whole-class feedback (see Table 11.7).

When marking essay-style questions as a teacher, we can lift examples of answers which have been completed to varying degrees of detail and success and share them (anonymously) with the class as part of whole-class feedback.

There are varying ways this can be done, either with a teacher-analysis of the answer (as in the example below), or as part of self and peer marking (as above) where students highlight the differences between their answer and the three example answers.

This extract is taken from the final movement of Mendelssohn's Violin Concerto in E minor.

a *Describe what you hear, with reference to instrumentation, melody, harmony, pitch, rhythm, articulation, tonality, tempo, and texture. [18]*

b *This extract is taken from a piece of music written during the Romantic Era. Give an example of a Romantic Era feature heard in the music. [2]*

Table 11.7 An example of 'good, better, best' answers

Description/ Marks	Model answer	Marking comments
Good 4 marks	The music features violin and orchestra (1).	Basic description of the instrumentation, melody, and rhythmic features.
	The melody is mostly stepwise (1).	No reference to the Romantic Era.
	The melody is high pitched (1).	
	The melody has both short and long notes (1).	

(Continued)

Table 11.7   An example of 'good, better, best' answers *(Continued)*

Description/ Marks	Model answer	Marking comments
Better 9 marks	The music features solo violin and orchestra (1).	Basic description of the instrumentation, melody, and rhythmic features.
	The melody is mostly stepwise (1) with ascending (1) and descending (1) patterns.	Some additional information given with basic musical terminology used.
	The violin melody is high pitched (1).	No reference to the Romantic Era.
	There are also flutes playing at the same time as the solo violin (1).	
	The melody has both short and long notes (1).	
	The music is in a major key (1) and is a fast tempo. (1)	
Best 21 marks	The solo violin (1) is accompanied by an orchestra (1).	More detailed description of instrumentation and melodic shape, using specific music terminology.
	The solo violin melody is mostly conjunct (1), both ascending (1) and descending (1) and features sequences (1).	Specific descriptions of timbre, appropriate to each instrument.
	The solo violin is mostly high pitched (1) and the flutes play in harmony (1) with the violin in places.	Specific rhythmic terminology used with accurate descriptions of the placement of these rhythms, relative to other rhythms.
	The melody is made up of mostly short notes (1) which are bouncy, dotted notes (1). These are then followed by long, legato (1) notes.	Appropriate musical terminology used for tonality, texture, and tempo.
	The solo violin plays high pitched (1) pizzicato (1) notes, as does the orchestral strings (1).	Links what is heard to the Romantic Era with a specific example.
	Both solo and orchestra strings play both pizzicato and arco (1) in the piece.	
	The tonality is Major (1), the tempo is vivace (1) and the texture is melody with homophonic accompaniment (1).	
	The solo violin alternates quickly between low-pitched arco notes (1) and high-pitched pizzicato (1) in a virtuosic fashion (1), common in the Romantic Era.	

References

Dexter, D. D., Park, Y. J., & Hughes, C. A. (2011). A meta–analytic review of graphic organizers and science instruction for adolescents with learning disabilities: implications for the intermediate and secondary science classroom. *Learning Disabilities Research & Practice*, 26(4), 204–213.

12

Physical education

Adam Goodwin

Introduction

'It's only PE. Grab some balls, bibs, cones, a whistle, and job done', I hear as I roll my eyes, again. 'It must be easy teaching PE', my colleague confidently proclaims. Do I align their misconceptions or do I allow them to continue with their outdated, completely disillusioned thoughts? I chose the latter. It is true that we do need many of these resources and many pupils do enjoy PE, but that, as I am sure you would agree is the tiniest tip of the iceberg. In my experience, many PE teachers become school leaders. Is that because PE teaching is 'so easy' or is it because of the teamwork, leadership, tactical thinking and adaptability qualities (to name a few) many of us possess? To be an effective PE teacher, as with any effective teacher, it requires a whole bucket-full of strategies stemmed from evidence and experience. Nobody is the fountain of knowledge, but having an adaptive, strategic, evidence-based approach to teaching will certainly help fill that bucket. Teaching is nothing new, but the way we do this has developed and cycled since the times of Egypt's Middle Kingdom more than 2000 years BC. The difference now is that there is so much more evidence to support how we teach and what we teach, derived from our increasing understanding of how we learn. Do we PE teachers listen to that little voice inside our heads which constantly evaluates and informs our actions? Or do we keep doing the same things that we have always done and always got the same results? Are we metacognitive? Do we enable our pupils to demonstrate metacognition? If it is not broke, why fix it, right? Wrong! Even if it is not broke, why should not we try to improve it? Afterall, you did buy them new trainers, even though your others still had plenty of life in them...

Below I will explore a range of metacognitive strategies linked to PE, across a mix of both practical and theory lessons.

Planning

Let us first consider strategies relating to planning.

Strategy evaluation

As a PE teacher, I have found that we, and our pupils, are generally aware of what a certain outcome looks like: a serve in tennis, a goal in football, a high jump in athletics and so on and so forth, but are they strategically planning their journey to this destination? A pupil may think 'well, you just throw the ball in the air and hit is with the racket, or you just jump over the bar', well... yes, but also no. Many of these are serial skills and have 'chunked' sections to them. If we say to our pupils, 'here is a ball and a racket, you're going to stand at this service line and try land the ball into the other service box', this may happen – it may even happen three times in a row – but is it effective to apply to a competitive situation?

As PE teachers, we often model a skill or an outcome, or at least have a pupil do this, without a conscious thought of 'if I model this like X then pupils will have a clearer understanding of what Y will look like'. It is just what we do. I sometimes ask pupils to identify which is the correct technique/model and for them to discuss in pairs or working groups, for them to feedback to me. After we have identified the correct way a skill should look, then what about how it feels, how it sounds, etc., taking into consideration more that one of our senses? As a PE teacher, and potentially an athlete too, you know when a skill you are performing feels and sounds right. Can we have our pupils reflect in this way too? Do we have 'Sir, when I played that golf shot, it vibrated up my arm and didn't feel right' or 'Miss, when I tried to smash the shuttlecock, it sounded like it hit the metal.' If that is the case, then brilliant, we have learners who are reflective and using the self-check (Mosston & Ashworth, 2002) approach, enabling pupils to evaluate their own performance against a set criterion, but pupils must be taught this first. When you were younger, you did not automatically know that a comma in the wrong place would change how some text is read, so why would you expect pupils to have a pre-determined idea of how something feels and sounds?

Is there other way we can arrive at the criteria we need to be successful in this skill? Do we consider the strengths and weaknesses of performing a skill a certain way? Running up to the high jump and not taking off from your outside foot would have consequences. Discuss. Could a basketballer shoot over the back of their heads? Yes, of course, but is it an effective method? No. Offering questions like this to our pupils and hosting short discussions about the right and wrong way to perform a skill will enable pupils to reflect on their own performance of the skill or in a competition, and ultimately decrease the learning time.

Knowledge organisers

Have you ever tried to create a knowledge organiser for practical topics? Have you ever even thought about it?

Across my time teaching, I have developed what I would say is 'an experienced head' for GCSE PE and BTEC Sport, in its many different formats. Many courses differ yet have many similarities. I have recently explored setting individual learning tasks (homework) for my pupils which require them to scour the GCSE PE Specification for the three sports they are wanting to be assessed in (yes, I did direct them to the source). They then produced knowledge organisers of the sports and skills in which they would be assessed in, linking it to the marking criteria, how they would achieve it, and what their strengths and areas for improvement are in those sports/skills. Why would I do this, you may ask? What would be the benefit of having someone of a very high level do this? They can already perform to the highest level, and you know that. Well, yes I do. But it is more than 'I know the skills and I know I can perform them', it is about self-reflection and an evaluation of this is where I currently am, and this is where I need to be. Should both answers be the same ('I am currently where I need to be'), then this is also fine, because this can inform other self-reflective practices such as their coursework (which I appreciate differs across exam boards), but the knowledge of I can do this well and this not so well allows the pupil to delve deeper into this and think, 'why do I do this well?', 'is it because of my skill?' If so, then what within that skill do they do well? Are there any areas for improvement? Mapping out this information is powerful. Whether it be practical performance in GCSE PE or Key Stage 3 practical topics matters not, it is the ability to acknowledge key skills/knowledge and identify what they have done well and/ or how to plug those gaps.

Knowing you caught a fish is good. Knowing how you caught the fish is power.

Problem-solving grids

Problem-solving grids are brilliant for those longer answer questions or developing coursework responses in Key Stage 4. I tend to use these grids when we build and model responses together. As we develop this, it is important to ensure autonomy of the child, while maintaining a clear, appropriate structure. Having pupils as part of the process is key to owning their own responses and making their knowledge effective to application. It is very easy for us to offer an exam question to a pupil, and some will be able to identify exactly what is required of them from transferrable skills developed previously, but others will not. Some pupils will struggle to comprehend what the task is asking, what the key chunks of information are and, potentially, what is irrelevant. If we have a question such as 'Thomas is a long-jumper and Edward is a 100 m sprinter. Both athletes train four times per week and represent their county at regional athletics events. Eval-uate the methods of training both would need to use to progress their training'. Now, we would look to identify the key information such as their events (100 m and long jump), the frequency of their training and the requirement to evaluate the training methods. We could then look to identify which training methods each athlete would require (e.g., acceleration training, power training, etc.) then those which they may not, or at least in limited volume (e.g., continuous training). The purpose of this is for the pupil to show what they know and how to apply it. This is all a part of the comprehension quadrant.

Connections would then be made to times when similar question have been encountered. 'Three-weeks ago, we had a retrieval question on training methods for a footballer, when we evaluated the response to that, is there any information that we could transfer and apply to this situation?'. Well, yes. We know that a footballer will also be using speed, power, etc., so we can use some of this information and transfer the skills we developed there to this. As important as it is to identify the key content, it is also fundamental to acknowledge what went wrong. Were there any misconceptions? We can use these to our strengths.

Strategies are important when a pupil is coming to write their response. We want them to have a strategic thought process about the outlay of the content. Do we randomly regurgitate the information that we have and hope that it makes sense? Or do we have our pupils think about the number of training methods they wish to write about, the necessity of effective and ineffective methods, the need to write about both athletes and where they are going to gain their marks? You will know yourself that pupils have an incredible ability to write a response which rewords the question and 'beats around the bush' rather than directly and effectively writing their response with essential information to gain marks.

Evaluation is key to inform future responses. We need feedback to provide our pupils with the strengths and areas to improve for their next questions. Not only does performing an evaluation inform pupils, but it does us too. We can reflect and think, 'that strategy didn't actually work' or, 'perhaps I taught that wrong' or, 'that went well, the pupils responded to our modelling effectively and that is something I will look to use again in the future, either again with this group or next years' cohort etc.'

It is key to remember that as effective this model is for Key Stage 4, it can also be applied to Key Stage 3. Admittedly, we probably would not give much, or in fact any time to writing this down, but we will still plan how we achieve our outcomes. We could use it for developing set-plays or tactics in a game situation. There are many different uses for this within PE, even if the implementation differs greatly.

Monitoring

Here are some metacognitive strategies relating to monitoring.

Warning signs

Warning signs come with experience, obviously. You do not know what to avoid without some level of prior knowledge, and that is what pupils need from you, your knowledge. You may be thinking, yes, that is why I am a teacher, to pass on my knowledge in a hope that pupils will effectively apply it to said situation, but there is a difference in knowledge of outcome and knowledge of process. For example, let us say you wanted to get from one town to another in your car: you know the main roads you should be taking, so surely that is enough? Well, what if you had knowledge that there is road works, or the speed had been reduced to 50 over a prolonged piece of road along that route, and you knew that there were some B roads which were much quicker as a diversion, surely you would take that? This is exactly what we are looking at here in PE. You know some of your new Year 7 group will pass the rugby ball without looking (and not in a stylish, proficient way), and that at least one pupil in your Key Stage 4 theory group will mix up agonistic, antagonist and antagonistic. So, what can we do to mitigate these, and any other issues we know are likely to arise? What do we do to prevent that from happening? Well, we may insert a conditioned practice to the lesson on passing, or provide ways to remember the key, confusing words: in an antagonistic pair, agonist is a shorter word, while antagonist is a longer word; the agonist shortens when it contracts, and the antagonist lengthens as it relaxes. Perhaps these and other (likely better) techniques are obvious, but they certainly help to mitigate misconceptions of our pupils, likely enabling them to succeed quickly or allowing us to identify and correct other misconceptions which we may not have a pre-determined knowledge of. Other tactics could include having pupils observe some prior material, which they could work to identify the problems or errors. I often find this is useful, as pupils then become more a part of the process, rather than just the task.

Flow maps

I would now like you to go and perform a forward roll. To do that, you should have two feet together, crouch, hands down, push with your feet, roll on to your shoulders, then on to your back, keep your chin tucked in along with your knees, plant your feet, then push up to stand back up without using your hands. Or a simple step-by-step visual/ model? I know which one I would rather use to help me perform and self or peer assess (British Gymnastics, 2021).

The use of flow maps is not to be confused with learning styles. This does not intend to show a switch from 'auditory to visual', as there is very little evidence of 'VAK learning styles' being effective or necessary at all. The EEF state 'there is very limited evidence for any consistent set of learning 'styles' that can be used reliably to identify the learning needs of young people. Instead, teachers hoping to target learning effective might consider other teaching and learning practices.' (EEF, 2021). The use of flow maps is more about being able to demonstrate the journey from A to B or from initiation to completion. The pros and cons of these though are: this strategy is great for a serial skill when there is a clear routine to follow e.g. in a gymnastics forwards roll, a tennis serve, a golf swing, etc., although may not always serve a purpose in more creative or open-ended skills with more autonomy. It could be a model with ingredients which have a systemic approach, the necessities if you like. If your pupils are answering an evaluation exam question, you may not decide to give them each piece of information which would contribute to the whole response, but you would probably give them the tools and skills to answer the question effectively.

Content checklists

We all love a checklist – something to cross off to say task done, to show progression. To-do lists, shopping lists, etc. These all allow for systematic acknowledgement that we are getting closer to the product and completion of the task. Teachers use this protocol all the time in schemes of work, observations, QA reviews, assessment, data input, to name a few. A content checklist is very much the same, but one that we can offer to our pupils, or at least enable our pupils to develop themselves. We need our pupils to get from A to Z. Pupils can identify where they are now and can see the end goal of what they need to achieve, but what about b, c, d, e, f... you get my drift. Sometimes there may only be one or two parts to a successful response to a task, but what about when there are more? When skills or responses require multiple levels of input. Ok, so, some examples... running – a simple, continuous skill. Not many teaching points here. A 5-metre pass in football. Get the ball from me to my partner successfully. Give or take five simple steps that most pupils will pick up relatively quickly, if they have not already mastered this at an early age. The checklist might include balancing your body, using the instep of your foot, non-kicking foot placement, etc., but overall, relatively easy, memorable steps to become autonomous with the skill quite quickly. Then we have complex, serial skills; the tennis serves, the gymnastic vaults and javelin throws. These cannot simply be taught by using a few 'steps to success' (not effectively at least), but through a timely developmental, cognitive process. To learn these skills effectively with a consistent outcome, skills need to be taught, then developed, then added to, then taught again and so forth, hence why we do not only train in sports once, otherwise everyone would be a master. The checklists that we provide our pupils with or expect them to recall effectively will take a while longer to become autonomous, but having the ability to 'check off' each smaller skill within the larger skill shows progression, encourages motivation and allows for consistency.

Evaluation

This section looks at metacognitive strategies for evaluation.

Answering directed questions

Pupils are not always able to reflect effectively. They might look back on what they have done and be very outcome focused. Even if they consider the performance or process, it may not always be clear to them what the key strategical elements of a task or development of a skill were. This is where we can support them further. Pupils are children with immature minds. Because of this, pupils can focus on questions such as 'did I do well?', 'did I win?', 'did I score?', etc. But if we can transform those questions to: Why did we win? Which skills did I use to be successful? Did I employ a strategic approach? Which criteria did I meet and not meet? What would I do differently next time? What would I do the same? Why? These questions can be used in an array of learning situations. We can use them as well as reflective practice for our teaching. Was my lesson mostly successful? Yes/no, why? Pupils did not achieve the grades I predicted in their mock exams. Why? What would I do differently and the same next time? It all mirrors. Any reflective practice can be adapted to a variety of situations.

In a basketball lesson with Y7, we might look at shooting. I generally like to have this early in my scheme of work, mostly because of the overhead throws kids love to do. And no matter how many times you tell them that it is poor practice and you should be doing it this way, there is the one pupil who gets it in, and they all go sprinting around the hall like they have just won the FA Cup. It does not do much for your recommendation. You know what I mean. When I have taught shooting in basketball, it is worth asking questions like: Were you evenly balanced? Where did you aim for? – be more specific – you were shooting from an angle; did you aim for the hoop or for the top corner of the backboard square? Did you shoot from the shoulder? – flip that around – what techniques did you use to shoot? What do you think you did here that made it a successful shot, in comparison to those you missed before? Some pupils may need a set list of criteria, like what I go on to mention below in the self/peer marking strategy, or previously mentioned in the content checklist section.

In a theory lesson, it is a very powerful tool to make comparisons. Show two (or more) models to the same answer on the board, or as hand out resources. Have pupils mark them with or without a mark scheme. Which response is best and why? What strategies have they used? What mark would you give them? Why? If it can be improved, what would you due to improve it? – now what is the mark? Could you steal any of the techniques used here for your own response to a slightly different question? You could keep this on the same topic, just adapted. Rather than a question like 'evaluate an endomorphs suitability to athletics', let us change it to 'evaluate an ectomorph's suitability to athletics'.

Having pupils as reflective learners helps them become strategic learners. With this strategy, the why is vital. Expecting pupils to evidence their response is vital.

Self/peer marking

This metacognitive strategy is great in so many ways. Let us begin with practical lessons.

Pupils do not generally have something written to mark, but what they can do is give effective feedback and coaching to their peers or even themselves. Having pupils teach each other is one of the best ways to embed learning for themselves. Let us take a badminton serve, for example. It may be that the teacher has demonstrated, highlighted the key teaching points, checked for knowledge through retrieval practices, etc., then you find that a pupil still cannot serve effectively. We can have a peer coach them through what they need to improve. Is it the stance? Is the pupil displaying what I call 'train track feet'? Parallel feet to the majority. Or are they in a suitable stance to transfer their weight? Do they have a slight tilt at the hips? Are they holding the shuttle feathers with their index finger and thumb? Pupils can peer evaluate and self-evaluate this, then look to correct it. What about when they are connecting with the shuttle, but it is going wayward? The peer may identify that when they are striking the shuttle, the racket follows through across the performers body, and therefore sending the shuttle in the wrong direction. There are many different coaching examples within sports that peers can undertake. Pupils can also use technology to record their performances and self-assess. By taking part in these activities, it removes the outcome focus and imparts more of a process focus. If each ingredient is added correctly and at the right time, the outcome is more likely to be successful. It is the whole knowledge of performance, rather than knowledge of result information, which helps pupils, and us, to develop skills.

In theory lessons, the opportunity and ability for pupils to review their own or a peer's work can be very powerful. Pupils may work from a mark scheme, which is perhaps the more common method, but how about having a list of common misconceptions? Ideally these would have been pre-determined and shared in the planning stages of the task, but sometimes pupils still repeat these misconceptions or allow you to discover new misconceptions. If pupils are able to review and feedback to their peer or themselves about the strengths and areas to improve, then this method of metacognition is very useful.

PMI grids

I think these grids are a great reflective and planning tool in both theory and practical, for both participants and non-participants/peer assessment, although I do believe they lack one thing which I will explain.

I am sure you are following a similar thought pattern to me when I first saw these, thinking that you can instantly see where they would fit in with an exam question. You prepare a response together, pupils complete it, you give them the mark scheme, they identify some of the things they have done well, not so well and something they found interesting that they could adapt to be more accurate or effective. I began using these, or an adaption of, with non-participants in practical PE lessons to help pupils coach and reflect on performances. Having a pupil assess another pupil with the PMI criteria and then feedback is powerful, assuming they know what they are looking for. I used PDM – plus, developing, minus – as a Venn diagram (see below). I feel like having pupils identify a skill or strategy which is useful but not effective yet was great to develop conversations and provided an expectation for pupils to provide the all-important why (Figure 12.1).

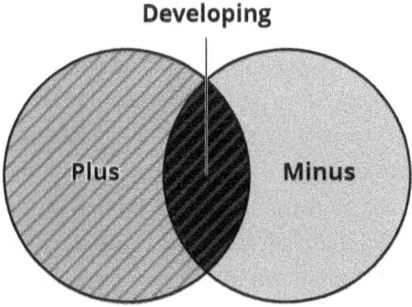

Figure 12.1 The PDM model

As I earlier alluded to, this method can be very effective for planning too. We teachers know it is imperative to be reflective also, and to use pupil voice and misconceptions to inform our own planning. Having pupils use these PMI (or PDM) grids can enable us to get a clearer understanding of how pupils perceived their strengths and areas to improve.

Also, pupils can use this to examine exemplar or research material. I found this to be effective on a nine-mark GCSE PE question – particularly the PMIs for theory. I handed pupils two exemplar answers, both of similar length – as pupils generally assume an answer with more quantity deserved a greater grade, yet one was given six marks and the other nine. Then with the grid and mark scheme, pupils worked together to read sieve out what they felt were the pluses, minuses and anything interesting. It sparked interesting discussion and helped to plan effective responses.

References

British Gymnastics. (2021, April 30). *From Proficiency Awards to Rise Gymnastics*. Available at: https://www.british-gymnastics.org/articles/rise-gymnastics/how-do-gymnasts-transfer-from-proficiency-awards-to-rise

Education Endowment Foundation [EEF]. (2021). *Learning Styles*. Available at: https://educationendowmentfoundation.org.uk/education-evidence/teaching-learning-toolkit/learning-styles

Mosston, M., & Ashworth, S. (2002). *Teaching Physical Education* (6th ed.). New York: Macmillan College Publishing Company.

13

Computing

Jonathan Usherwood

Introduction

Computing is a unique subject that blends logic, creativity and technical skill – but because of its focus on things like programming languages and algorithms, it is easy to assume that metacognitive strategies do not really have a place. Lessons often concentrate on solving problems or learning specific skills, and there is not always room to step back and think about how students are learning or how they are thinking through problems.

But metacognition is actually a huge part of what makes students successful in computing. Whether they are debugging a tricky section of code, planning a solution to a complex problem or trying to explain how a computer works, students are constantly making decisions about what they know, what they need to find out and how best to move forward. These are all metacognitive processes – even if they are not always recognised as such.

This chapter will explore how metacognitive strategies can be woven into computing lessons in a way that feels natural and useful. We will focus mainly on Key Stage 4, where students start to face more complex and abstract ideas, and where thinking about how they think can make a real difference. Whether it is writing pseudocode, analysing trace tables or preparing for theory exams, metacognition can help students work more independently, reflect more deeply and ultimately feel more confident in what they are doing.

Planning

Let us now look at metacognitive strategies relating to planning.

Graphic organisers

Visual organisers can be incredibly effective in computing by helping pupils understand complex concepts, organise information and enhance their problem-solving skills.

There are many examples of graphic organisers that can be used in computing teaching; in this chapter, we will consider two – concept maps and the Frayer model.

Concept maps

Concept maps are essentially visual tools that help organise and represent knowledge. At their core, they consist of concepts connected by labelled links, forming statements or propositions. In computing lessons, concept maps can capture the expertise of subject specialists, educators and learners. This means that they are incredibly useful for planning, teaching, learning and assessment.

In computing lessons, pupils can use concept maps to organise and visualise their knowledge. They can map out how different programming constructs like loops, conditionals, and functions interact, making it easier to understand these concepts. Working in groups to create and discuss concept maps also encourages collaboration. Teachers can use these maps to assess understanding and spot any gaps in knowledge. This interactive approach not only makes lessons more engaging but also helps pupils retain complex computing concepts better. One way of encouraging this use is to visit the concept map as part of every lesson, for example, a 'plenary' where pupils summarise the lesson's work or during a 'do now' where pupils recall the information from the previous lesson. There are plenty of online tools to support this work and speed up the process. Another technique is to give pupils a partially complete concept map, or a fully complete concept map, depending on how much control you want over the tool as well as what you want to use the tool for.

Below is an example of a concept map that could be used to teach networks at GCSE Computer Science (Figure 13.1).

The Frayer model

The Frayer model (Figure 13.2) is a very useful graphic organiser tool for use in computing because it helps pupils break down complex concepts into manageable parts and let us be honest there are plenty of these, especially in the way of new key terms that they might not have been introduced to in their prior learning. By using the model, your pupils can clearly define a concept, identify its characteristics and distinguish between examples and non-examples. This structured approach is crucial in computing, where understanding precise definitions and characteristics is essential for problem-solving and programming.

Key word quizzing

By incorporating keyword quizzing into the computing curriculum, you can significantly enhance pupils' retention and understanding of essential terminology. Keyword quizzing reinforces the language of computing, ensuring that pupils become fluent in the vocabulary necessary to grasp more complex concepts. Regular quizzes can be designed to progressively challenge pupils, moving from basic definitions to applying terms in practical scenarios.

This method not only aids memorisation but also encourages active engagement with the material. When pupils must recall and use key terms in various contexts, their

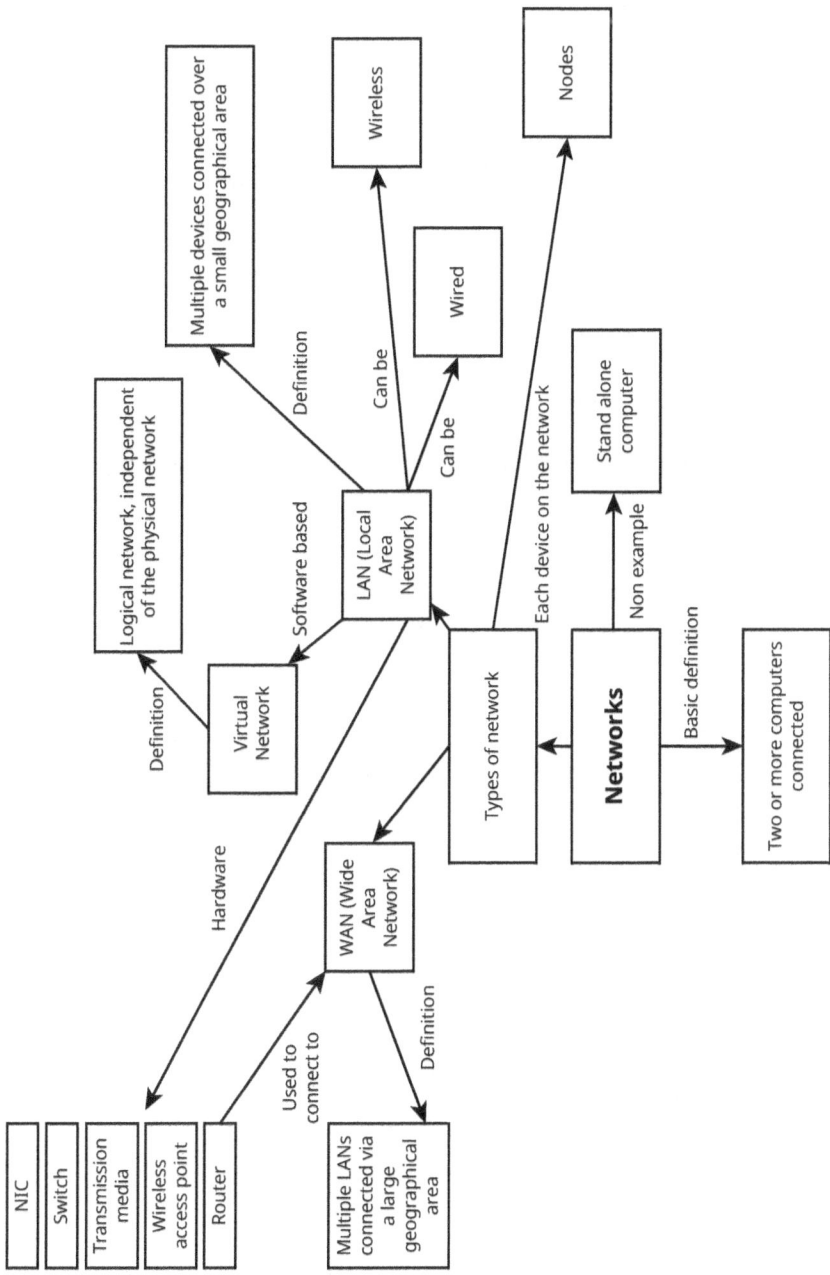

Figure 13.1 A concept map to teach networks

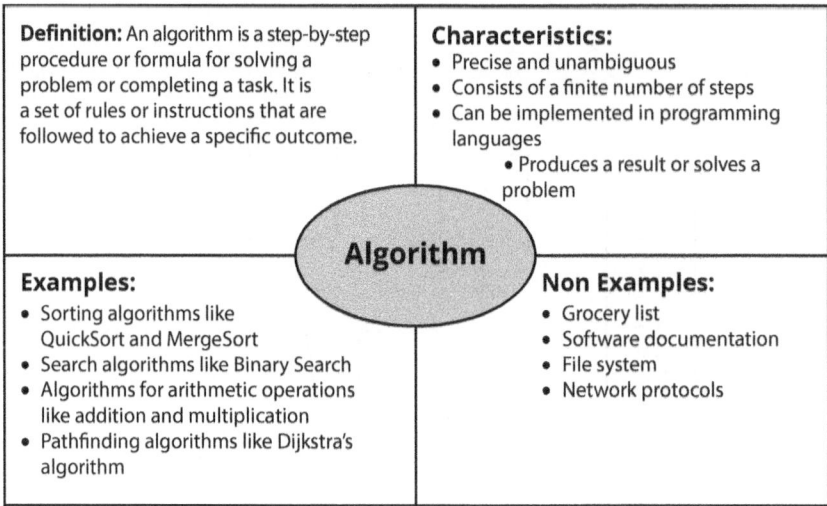

Figure 13.2   An example of a completed Frayer model for the concept of an algorithm

cognitive skills are sharpened, and their confidence in the subject matter is bolstered. Effective quizzing can also highlight areas where pupils may need further clarification or support, allowing for targeted interventions and personalised learning strategies. Remember to utilise the technology you have available to generate keyword quizzes. While it is a good idea for you to quiz your pupils through questioning, they can also do this in pairs or individually using software to give them feedback. There are plenty of free tools available on the internet that you can easily access in your computing lessons.

Exam question analysis

Exam question analysis is an extremely powerful tool in any subject, but especially in computing, coupled with the fact that the majority of your teaching time, you will have access to computer rooms, so incorporating technology into this process becomes a bit of a 'no brainer'. There are plenty of exam question analysis tools on the internet, and with a little bit of tinkering, you can make yourself an interactive, conditionally formatted, all-singing all-dancing spreadsheet. Not that it has to be this complex, simplicity is sometimes more effective, but the point is that you can give this interactive tool to your pupils to play with, to see how far from a mark boundary, what would have happened if they had got one more mark on this question and so on, and this should be encouraged. More crucially, pupils can see a glimpse of where their weaker and stronger areas were on the exam, and so they then know which areas of the curriculum they need to focus on. Moreover, as a computing teacher, you can then tailor your lessons, interleaving do nows to reflect these areas that require more time, or you can identify the individual pupils that require extra attention in these topic areas.

Let us consider the following example (Table 13.1).

Table 13.1   A Table showing six pupils' scores for five questions taken from an exam

	Q1 – Algorithms/4	Q2 – Network protocols/layers/3	Q3 – Binary conversion/2	Q4 – Hexadecimal conversion/2	Q5 – Coding solution/6
Pupil 1	3	1	2	2	4
Pupil 2	3	1	2	2	5
Pupil 3	3	0	2	2	6
Pupil 4	4	1	2	1	2
Pupil 5	2	2	2	0	3
Pupil 6	1	1	1	0	2

From the snapshot above, it is quite clear from an overview which topics need some whole class focus on, and from a pupil level, which topics certain pupils need to focus on. You could then take this a step further through a bespoke analysis so that each pupil is given a personalised list of the above. Pupils can then analyse each question that has been identified as a weakness to see where improvements can be made, and equally as important they can look at the ways in which they gained their highest marks.

Monitoring

Let us now consider metacognitive strategies relating to monitoring.

Checklists

Through the teaching of computing, you will teach a considerable amount of procedural knowledge. To support this knowledge, a checklist can be massively beneficial. Checklists can be either teacher-generated or pupil-created, each offering unique benefits. When you introduce a new concept, for example, programming in Python or debugging techniques, you could provide a checklist outlining critical phases such as problem definition, pseudocode writing, coding, testing and final debugging. This structured guidance will scaffold your pupil learning, providing a concrete reference to ensure key steps are not overlooked.

By encouraging pupils to write their own checklists, they engage in planning and self-monitoring. Suppose a pupil is working on a web design project, their checklist might start with conceptualising and wireframing, then progress through creating the HTML structure, adding CSS for styling, and finally testing the site's functionality. By personalising this process, pupils cultivate a sense of ownership over their learning journey, building essential project management and self-evaluation skills.

Effective checklists have a chronological structure that mirrors the logical flow of computing tasks. This ensures that learners approach problems methodically, reducing errors and promoting efficiency. For example, imagine a computing class focused on building a basic calculator application. Pupils can create a checklist that begins with defining user requirements, proceeds through designing the user interface and moves to coding the addition, subtraction, multiplication, and division functions. Testing each function individually and then as a whole system would be the final stages. This checklist serves as both a guide and a reflective tool, enabling pupils to track their progress and address challenges systematically.

Practical example for a lesson

For a lesson on creating a simple Python programme, a checklist could include:

1 Define the problem.
2 Outline required inputs and expected outputs.
3 Write pseudocode for each step.
4 Translate pseudocode into Python code.
5 Run initial tests and record results.
6 Debug and revise code.
7 Perform final testing and documentation.

By following such a checklist, pupils gain a structured pathway to work through each programming stage, fostering critical thinking and boosting their confidence with each completed milestone.

Task success criteria

Using checklists in computing can be highly beneficial especially when completing projects, something you are very likely to encounter. They help pupils stay organised, ensure all key criteria are met and provide a clear structure for complex tasks. Checklists enable pupils to self-assess their progress, receive immediate feedback, and avoid missing important elements. This approach is particularly useful in projects like website creation, where multiple components need to be integrated seamlessly.

Task: Creating a simple website

Here is an example checklist to ensure all key criteria are met in a website project:
   Task Criteria/Marking Rubric:

1 **HTML Structure**: Ensure the website has a clear and correct HTML structure, including <!DOCTYPE html, <html>, <head>, and <body> tags.
2 **Title and Metadata**: Include a meaningful title and appropriate metadata in the <head> section.
3 **Content**: Add relevant content such as headings, paragraphs, images, and links.
4 **CSS Styling**: Apply CSS to style the website, including layout, colours, fonts, and spacing.
5 **Navigation**: Implement a navigation bar with links to different sections or pages.
6 **Responsiveness**: Ensure the website is responsive and looks good on different devices (e.g., desktop, tablet, and mobile).
7 **Accessibility**: Include accessibility features such as alt text for images and proper use of semantic HTML tags.

8 **Functionality**: Ensure all links and interactive elements work correctly.
9 **Code Quality**: Write clean, well-organised, and commented code.

Monitoring Strategy

- **Teacher/Pupil Checklist**:
  1 HTML Structure:
     ○ Doctype declaration is present.
     ○ HTML, head, and body tags are correctly used.
  2 Title and Metadata:
     ○ Title is descriptive and relevant.
     ○ Metadata tags (e.g., charset, viewport) are included.
  3 Content:
     ○ Headings and paragraphs are used appropriately.
     ○ Images have alt text.
     ○ Links are functional and relevant.
  4 CSS Styling:
     ○ CSS is linked or embedded correctly.
     ○ Styles are applied to layout, colours, fonts, and spacing.
  5 Navigation:
     ○ Navigation bar is present.
     ○ Links in the navigation bar work correctly.
  6 Responsiveness:
     ○ Website adjusts layout for different screen sizes.
     ○ Media queries are used if necessary.
  7 Accessibility:
     ○ Alt text is provided for all images.
     ○ Semantic HTML tags are used (e.g., <header>, <main>, <footer>).
  8 Functionality:
     ○ All links and interactive elements are tested and working.
  9 Code Quality:
     ○ Code is clean and well-organised.
     ○ Comments are used to explain sections of the code.

Warning signs

In teaching computing, there are a lot of key misconceptions that can arise, especially if you consider the preconceptions of pupils, for example, the concept of programming being particularly difficult and only suitable for the 'select few'. In reality, as we know programming can be accessed by everyone, it all depends on the way they are introduced and taught. The following is an example of a warning sign strategy that could be used in the teaching of programming skills where we look at what could be said by the teacher and the pupil:

Teacher: "Alright class, today we're going to work on a programming task, investigating different types of iteration. In our previous lesson we used the Predict, Run, and Investigate parts of PRIMM to look at different loops. Today we will be modified the code and making our own versions. Before we start, let's talk about some 'warning signs' or 'red flags' that might indicate something has gone wrong in your code. These are common mistakes that you should watch out for. If you spot any of these, it means you need to go back and check your work."

Pupil: "What kind of warning signs should we look for with loops?"

Teacher: "Great question! Here are a few examples:

1 **Infinite Loops:** If your program seems to be stuck and never finishes running, you might have an infinite loop. This often happens if the loop's exit condition is never met. For example, in a while loop, make sure the condition will eventually become false.

2 **Off-by-One Errors:** These occur when your loop iterates one time too many or one time too few. For example, if you are using a for loop to iterate over an array, make sure your loop boundaries are correct.

3 **Incorrect Loop Conditions:** If your loop condition is incorrect, your loop might not run the expected number of times. Double-check your conditions to ensure they accurately reflect the logic you intend.

4 **Uninitialised Variables:** If you are using a variable in your loop condition or within the loop, make sure it is properly initialised before the loop starts. Otherwise, you might get unexpected results or errors."

Pupil: "What should we do if we see one of these warning signs?"

Teacher: "If you spot a warning sign, don't panic! It's a signal to go back and review your code step-by-step. For example, if you have an infinite loop, check your loop condition and make sure it will eventually be false. If you have an off-by-one error, review your loop boundaries and adjust them as needed. The key is to catch these issues early so you can fix them before you run out of time."

Pupil: "That makes sense. Can we start coding now?"

Teacher: "Yes, go ahead and start your task. Remember to keep an eye out for those warning signs. If you get stuck, raise your hand and I'll come help you. Good luck!"

While this might not reflect the exact dialogue between yourself and your pupils, you should be able to get the picture of how you can use the warning signs to support your pupils.

Evaluation

Here are some metacognitive strategies relating to evaluation.

Self/peer marking

Marking in any subject is a huge contributor to teacher workload, and peer and self-marking in computing can be great to reduce some of this marking, especially with homework. If pupils are reviewing each other's work digitally, which is highly likely, for example, if they are reviewing coding work, it may be useful for pupils to save different versions, for example, 'my programv1', 'myprogramv2', 'myprogramv3', etc., which can be useful in programming to allow for version control and for work such as graphic design, as it slows pupils to showcase work including developmental drafts. (Lau, 2017). Another technique is to allow pupils to use different coloured font when reviewing work. You can also allow pupils to move places around the classroom, for example, 'move 2 spaces clockwise'. Even something as simple as this can motivate pupils as it will probably be different to the everyday nature of the class, just remember to pre-plan this activity.

Pair programming is a brilliant strategy that incorporates peer work. In paired programming, two pupils work together on a programming task. One pupil acts as the 'driver' who writes the code, while the other is the 'navigator', who reviews the code and provides feedback. They switch roles regularly. This method allows for continuous self and peer assessment as pupils give each other feedback throughout the task. It mirrors industry practices and has been shown to reduce errors (NCCE, n.d.).

During any form of self/peer marking, it is important to provide pupils with some form of rubric, especially when assessing programming tasks. This helps pupils focus on the learning objectives and provides clear expectations for the assessment process. You may also want to consider anonymous feedback to encourage honest and constructive feedback. This can be done using screen-sharing software or tools like Google Classroom. By removing the personal element, pupils are more likely to provide genuine feedback that supports learning. You may just need to remind pupils to 'critique with kindness!'

Learning diaries

Learning diaries can be a powerful tool in the computing classroom, providing pupils with a structured way to reflect on their learning, track progress, and identify areas for improvement. By documenting their progress in programming skills, for example, pupils can note the concepts they have mastered, the challenges they faced and the strategies they used to overcome these challenges. There is nothing better than seeing that moment when a pupil solves a problem or learns new syntax to solve a coding problem. To be able to document this will enable the pupil to see that journey from start to finish, but they can also reference back to this if they encounter the problem again. It could be another week before that pupil programs again, and if they have their own reference point, this might enable them to progress in the next lesson. Once you have this as part of your routine, pupils will get used to filling out the learning journey, and this can be easily done either in books or through a 'digital learning diary'. Either way, it will be a huge benefit to their work in computing.

Having the ability to complete a digital learning diary can be incredibly beneficial, not only to you but also to the pupils. Firstly, they can be integrated with other educational tools and platforms, which allows your pupils to maintain their diaries online and include multimedia elements like screenshots of code, videos of their projects and links to resources. This makes the learning diary a rich, interactive tool for reflection and learning. You may also find that the teaching of some courses, especially in the information technology part of computing, requires pupils to keep some form of diary or log of their work. Not only is this a good metacognitive strategy, but you are also completing the required coursework, win win!

Let us look at the following example from a python programming lesson:

Example: Learning diary for a programming project

- Date: 13 December 2024
- Project: Creating a Simple Calculator in Python

Concepts Mastered:

- Learnt how to define functions in Python.
- Successfully implemented basic arithmetic operations (addition, subtraction, multiplication, and division).
- Understood the use of if-else statements for error handling (e.g., division by zero).

Challenges Faced:

- Struggled with syntax errors when defining functions.
- Had difficulty understanding how to handle user input and convert it to the correct data type.
- Encountered issues with the programme crashing when invalid input was provided.

Strategies Used:

- Referred to online Python documentation to understand function syntax.
- Used print statements to debug and trace errors in the code.
- Implemented try-except blocks to handle invalid input and prevent the programme from crashing.

Reflection:

- It was really satisfying to see the calculator work correctly after fixing the errors.
- Documenting each step helped me understand where I went wrong and how I fixed it.
- I realised the importance of handling user input carefully to make the programme more robust.

Next Steps:

- Explore more advanced features like adding a graphical user interface (GUI) to the calculator.

- Learn about more complex error handling techniques.
- Practice writing more functions to improve code modularity and reusability.

Multimedia Elements:

- Screenshots: Included screenshots of the code and the running programme.
- Videos: Recorded a short video demonstrating the calculator in action.
- Links: Added links to useful resources and tutorials that helped during the project.

PMI grids

As you are already aware, the PMI grid is an effective metacognitive strategy that encourages pupils to reflect on their learning experiences. By categorising their thoughts into successes (Plus), areas for improvement (Minus), and points of interest (Interesting), pupils can gain a deeper understanding of their progress and challenges. In a computing context, this strategy can be particularly valuable. For instance, after a lesson on computer networks, pupils can use the PMI grid to identify what concepts they grasped well, such as understanding the basic components of a network, what they found challenging, like configuring network settings, and what piqued their curiosity, such as the role of network security protocols. This reflective practice not only helps pupils consolidate their learning but also provides teachers with insightful feedback to tailor future lessons and address specific needs.

Let us look at an example below. The teacher has just taught an introduction to cyber security and used some brilliant resource to capture the imagination of their pupils. One of the pupils fills out the following PMI grid (Table 13.2).

Table 13.2 A PMI grid for computing

Plus (Successes)	Minus (Areas for Improvement)	Interesting (Points of Interest)
- Got the hang of the basic cybersecurity stuff, like keeping data safe and making sure it's accurate.	- Found the encryption algorithms super confusing.	- Really cool how hackers trick people using social engineering.
- Learnt about common cyber threats like phishing and malware.	- Struggled with setting up a basic firewall.	- Want to know more about ethical hacking and how to test security.
- Figured out how to make strong passwords and why multi-factor authentication is important.	- Need to get better at spotting and dealing with phishing scams.	- Interested in the different jobs you can get in cybersecurity.

As a teacher, you can then use the summaries of the grids to develop the planning for the next lesson(s). You may even want to utilise pupils completing this electronically so that you can gather the data and analyse it easily. Remember to utilise the technology!

Reference

Lau, W. (2017). *Teaching Computing in Secondary Schools, A Practical Handbook*. David Fulton.

National Centre for Computing Education [NCCE] (n.d.). *Pedagogy Quick Reads: Pair Programming Supports Learners to Produce Better Solutions to Complex Programming Problems*. https://static.teachcomputing.org/pedagogy/QR3-Pair-programming.pdf

14

Art

Lucy Williams

Introduction

Art is possibly the most metacognitive of all subjects, and art teachers across the country are delivering powerful learning episodes, successfully demonstrating metacognition through art making and learning about artists and makers. However, metacognition in art may look very different from other subjects. Niall McNulty stated, 'implementing metacognitive practices in the classroom is not a one-size-fits-all approach, and it varies across disciplines and educational levels' (McNulty, 2024).

Art is not a content-driven subject, and to put this into context, we should remember that GCSE Art is the only subject with no written exam; there are two non-examination assessment (NEA) components. Component 1 is 60% coursework, and Component 2 is worth 40%. It is an externally set assignment (ESA), sometimes colloquially called an 'exam project', with a period of preparatory studies on a given theme. Students will explore, research, experiment, design and plan their outcome, culminating in a 10-hour sustained focus under exam conditions to create their autonomous piece of original and creative art. A' Level is similar, including a written element: a piece of continuous prose forming part of Component 1 (some teachers may refer to this as an 'essay' or 'artist statement'). Component 2 is also like the GCSE ESA, and the sustained focus under exam conditions is 15 hours. These assignments demand students respond to the theme independently. It is the job of the art teacher to ensure students are ready to do this and our Key Stage 3 should prepare for and inform this (DfE, 2013a; DfE, 2013b). Both GCSE and A' Level Art are marked holistically; therefore, how we utilise metacognition from Key Stage 3, or perhaps even earlier, should support this process. For Key Stages 4 and 5 art, it is vital students can work independently. Creativity is a unique human trait and a valuable skill; it can sit hand in hand with critical thinking. Research has shown that creative problem-solving and creative thinking are encouraged through metacognitive training, and critical thinking demands metacognition as well as cognition (Jia et al., 2019).

Metacognition is often a subconscious process in art; many students just do it without thinking, making connections with prior learning to create ideas and that is okay. This is a creative and critical thinking process. However, we can make some of this invisible learning visible. There is no right or wrong answer in art – even spilling paint can lead to a 'happy accident'; it could create a beautiful abstract artwork or create a wonderful colour.

I recently started to 'label' some episodes of metacognition in my lessons. For instance, in a Key Stage 4 lesson on the theme War/Conflict, I asked students to think about an issue they would like to create a personal idea for a final piece. Many linked to a historical period they learnt about in History. Some looked at recent political events on the news, and some are looking at a medical condition they have. I told them this is your metacognition. They were all drawing on prior learning, and some of this learning did not take place in the art room. Their 'everyday knowledge, ideas, representations of the world and experiences can help them to learn the concepts in the subject' (Ofsted, 2023).

We should be mindful not to enforce whole school assessment and marking policies onto Art (and other practical subjects), as this drips down and can impact how we teach. Whole school teaching and learning approaches will support pedagogy, student progress and attainment when appropriately applied. Art might be delivered as a single lesson once a week at Key Stage 3, or perhaps as part of a carousel, meaning only 12 lessons a year in some schools, and subject content time could focus on delivering much of the learning through practical work and outcomes.

The re-labelling of images or visuals as 'dual coding' some years ago tells us students learn more when they learn information linked to an image. Art teachers have been using images, visuals, and symbols to support learning for decades, if not centuries. Visual communication and visual language are a vital means of human communication.

When I trained to teach over 20 years ago, we explored metacognition as 'learning to learn' and 'prior knowledge'. In art, and other practical subjects, students can learn in many ways. In art, learning is often haptic and experiential. Haptic learning is when students learn through a sense of touch – a hands-on-approach enables students to learn through artmaking. Factual knowledge on its own is not enough, and in many cases, art teachers will want to see the knowledge practically applied. It is not as useful if a student knows red and yellow make orange and cannot make a range of orange tones. They will need to apply that knowledge to the practical task and learn by experimenting, or indeed by play. Knowledge and learning in art history (and cultural context) can be demonstrated through writing but should also be seen applied to practical work; students demonstrate knowledge of a style practically by using it, or aspects of it, in their own artwork. Ideas or concepts may also be borrowed from artists or works of art, as can composition. This enables students to develop and make their own work. Many schools employ teacher-led curriculums, gradually releasing control, but often the reality is that this is only released for high-attaining and perhaps naturally talented students (Carney, 2024). Could teaching metacognition and making it visible support students to be more independent and autonomous?

Metacognition has an important role in developing young artists and students towards independent and sustained working in the classroom. If students cannot develop and plan their own ideas and execute them to their best ability, then they may not achieve the outcomes they are capable of and will struggle with the ESA element of GCSE and A Level. This chapter will focus on GCSE Art but draws on how Key Stage 3 prepares for this and how Key Stage 4 prepares for Key Stage 5. I teach GCSE Art, Craft, and Design, but these principles can be applied to any of the disciplines of art (fine art, three-dimensional art, textiles, graphics, and photography), i.e. a two-dimensional sketch could be a tester, a sample or a maquette in three-dimensional work (When I mention Key Stage 4, my reference point is GCSE; however, it will also apply to aspects of BTEC, NCFE, and Technical Certificates).

The following sections are written from my own experience and conversations with colleagues, and through art teacher networks, they aim to support and provide ideas to make metacognition more visible in the classroom. They are by no means an exhaustive list. Art teachers will know their cohort and context and will be selecting appropriate ways to support and will already be using some of these and other strategies to support students to know, remember and do more and support their progress while nurturing a love of art and creativity.

Planning

Let us now consider metacognitive strategies relating to planning.

Visual planning

Visual planning in art is metacognitive, often a process of thinking, looking at images or objects, annotating, selecting, sketching, putting images together, altering images, experimenting with materials; the list can go on. Students ideate differently. As a student, I preferred to find inspirational images and combine them with written notes before starting to design and plan a composition. I taught a student years ago who plannedthrough detailed drawings, diagrams and comic strips to work out his ideas, process and every step was visible (he seldom used written notes) clearly communicating his ideas. Other students may employ a range of techniques: collecting images, doodling, making notes, drawing and experimenting. At Key Stages 4 and 5, it is important to note that not all planning will look the same in the students' work and it should not. They should be making independent choices in their coursework, especially personal responses.

Visual planning can support communicating compositional, colour, style, material and technique choices. The basic diagram in Figure 14.1 is a simple illustration demonstrating that there is more than one compositional choice for a black circle on a white background. This is visual planning. Quick thumbnail visuals (could be sketches, collage, photographs) of the same content of a two-dimensional work with the same ingredients in different compositions will support many students develop ideas.

Essentially, planning in art should be seen. It should be visual; I do not mean it should not contain written comments or annotation. You should be able to look at a student's work and see their ideas and planning. I find this analogy helps students: 'think about how you write a story in English or an essay in any subject, by the time you finish, it will have a beginning, middle and end. When writing a story or essay, you may not start at

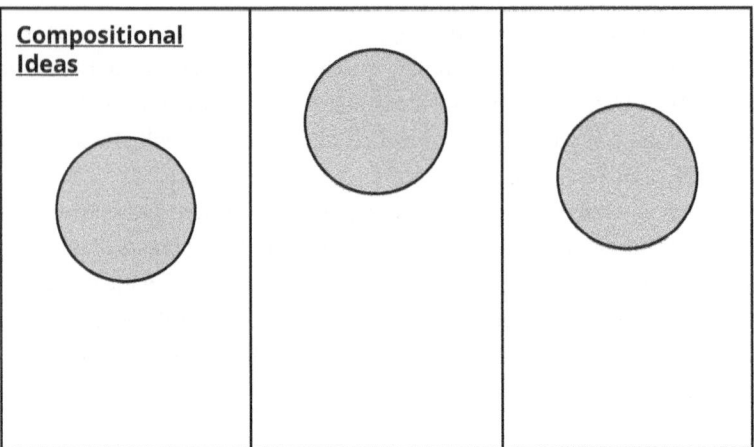

Figure 14.1   Three compositional choices for a black circle on a white background

the beginning and that's fine, it is okay in art too. Your thinking and planning should be visually seen and understood'. Art teachers will be teaching this in Key Stage 3 to ensure that by Key Stage 4, most students are aware of this process.

Graphic organisers as mind maps or brain dumps and image boards

Not every art teacher or student will find mind maps effective, but all artists jot down and sketch their ideas at some point. This can prevent cognitive overload. Personally, I find 'brain dumps' are a good way to encourage students across Key Stages 3 to 5 to think broadly about what they already know. A brain dump will look different for every student; some may write words, phrases, short sentences, doodles or sketches. Any of this is okay. In a GCSE project I deliver called 'War/Conflict', students brain dump their knowledge of a range of events and issues they are interested in at the beginning of the project (and again before designing a final piece). In the context of my school, what they know and experience is really varied. We are a multicultural and diverse community, and prior knowledge, experience and their own cultural capital is encouraged and explored if they want to. Students may find subheadings helpful to explore, but not necessary. I explain to students in all the key stages that their sketchbook is a place to record ideas, insights and observations, places for best work, experiments and recording information. Sometimes students do not value recording rough ideas, and reminding them that they get marks for showing working out in a maths exam helps them understand.

Image boards are a visual metacognitive process and can help students plan ideas, borrow or link ideas or styles together. Students should choose their own images. When using search engines, I encourage students to scroll down to select images rather than select the first examples. Students use visual reference materials to support planning ideas, materials, processes, techniques, content, etc. For our close-up GCSE Art project, I ask students to create an image board, finding a range of inspiring images of things close-up or zoomed in. I might make my own example or show examples from previous students' work. This hones observation skills and provides a visual reference. Students select from the domains of art, science, botany, geography, astronomy; the possibilities are endless, and metacognition supports choices. These images are used to inform ideas, support recording, developing, experimenting, exploring ideas, final piece planning or outcomes. When they select from a wealth of reference materials, students evidence metacognition through refining. This is often overlooked as a metacognitive act. If we make it visible as metacognition, it supports progress and increases independent thinking and ideas.

Planning documents

Planning documents are useful when students are planning a final piece or creating a personal outcome. Many art teachers utilise this as they encourage students to empty their brain on to the page ('brain dump'). It can be helpful to use the 'knowledge of' grid after this stage. Knowledge of task or brief is crucial to establish a starting point. Knowledge of self is not restricted to the curriculum but is often prior knowledge and what students already know (this is often a broad requirement in art). Knowledge of strategies refers to their knowledge of visual language, materials, process, and techniques. A formulised chart may not be the best way to communicate this planning stage as part of coursework, but it helps teach the strategy.

We develop, plan and create holistically in art. The holistic assessment structure of art means it is okay to start planning in any order (see Tables 14.1 and 14.2). The suggested headers below do not have to be completed in any order and can be evidenced and developed through written notes, sketching, taking their own photos, testing materials, image samples, or collage etc., which all support the design process. For Component 2, they should already know this strategy and employ it without the help chart (Pearson, 2016).

Table 14.1 Example 1 of a planning document in art

Knowledge of task	Knowledge of self	Knowledge of strategies
What do I need to do for this art task? How do I know?	What am I good at and is this okay for the task? How do I know?	What artists or makers, contextual inspiration will I borrow? What materials, techniques and processes will I use because I have experience of them already?
How much time do I have?	What areas interest me and why?	Why will I use these?
What size will it be (in the time I have)?		
What shape will it be?		
What are the requirements of the brief or assessment objective?	What ideas can I create from my previous artwork and prior knowledge across any appropriate area?	Do I want to explore any new artists, makers, materials, techniques, or processes that inspire me? If so, how will I know they are suitable?

Table 14.2 Example 2 of a planning document in art

Time to complete?	Scale	Object/issue/ content/main focus	Idea	Composition	Artist or contextual inspiration	Techniques	Material

Monitoring

Let us now explore metacognitive strategies relating to monitoring.

Warning signs

Art is a visual subject; students will visually and cognitively monitor their work. Making mistakes is part of learning. Although in art, we can take great joy in 'happy accidents', these can result in amazing artworks or ideas as well as learning. Art teachers will use warning signs when delivering practical demonstrations by intentionally making mistakes. For example, if I am teaching mono-printing with block ink, I might roll out too much ink and not put sufficient pressure when drawing so that students can see what happens if you use too much ink and not enough pressure. I would show my deliberate mistake and ask, 'are my lines and mark-making visible enough', 'why is this, what did I do wrong?'. A teacher may see a student make an error with a process or technique and show them how to correct it or refine their use of the material then stop the lesson and ask the student to tell the class what did not work well and explain how they refined or rectified it.

Checklists

Checklists are not necessary for all art tasks. I use two forms of checklists, one for learning new techniques or processes with numbered steps and checklists of tasks for GCSE students. I have noticed, in my setting, a growing number of Quality First Teaching strategies for SEND students include the use of checklists to support sequencing. I found numbering checklists, rather than bullet pointing, has supported our students follow the steps. Some art techniques have prescribed steps, especially where health and safety are concerned. Once students have followed the numbered steps to create the practical task, the list, haptic experience, and experiential learning help embed knowledge.

Teachers could check students' knowledge and understanding after a practical demonstration through their application of the practical work, their performance practically or perhaps a check list could be given out with a step missing or an incorrect word for students to correct. I give students checklists as a 'cloze' activity with words missing. I display written information incorrectly and see who finds the deliberate mistake first. These strategies can be used at any stage of a project as a reminder or recap.

At GCSE, I use checklists periodically to guide students in their catch-up time. I print a list of all class and homework set and tick against whether students' work is complete, incomplete or needs refining. Students can do this too. This checklist then supports independent work for catch-up or homework; students take control of their learning, developing independent habits of learning.

SCAMPER (Substitute, combine, adapt, modify/magnify, purpose, eliminate/minimise, and rearrange/reverse)

I am going to introduce SCAMPER here as a metacognitive strategy, and although it can be referenced as a brainstorming technique, I think it is so useful in art when students are stuck developing ideas (BBC BITESIZE, n.d.).

SCAMPER was originally developed by Alex Osborn in 1953 as a tool for advertising and was further developed by Bob Eberle in relation to teaching students to think creatively. You may see SCAMPER used in design and technology departments too. Some students will be able to pull ideas out of the air (this is metacognition at its fastest, isn't it?), but others find this tricky. SCAMPER will help. A student does not need to go through each letter of the acronym and can use them in any order. I display this (Table 14.3) as a poster in my classroom and have sheets with each letter as a prompt. The questions help when Key Stages 4 and 5 students are stuck experimenting, developing, recording, or exploring ideas.

Table 14.3   Applying SCAMPER as a metacognitive strategy in art

Substitute	Combine	Adapt	Modify	Purpose	Eliminate/ minimise	Reverse/ rearrange
How can you replace part of the artwork with something else?	How can you combine the artwork with something else? How can you merge your artwork or a section with something else?	How can you adapt the artwork by refining it? How can you adapt the artwork by changing the style, material, and technique?	How can you change the appearance or look? How can you make a visual change?	How can you use an object or the artwork for a different purpose?	How can you eliminate parts of the artwork or simplify it? How can you minimise the artwork to show a smaller scale?	How can you reverse or flip an image/artwork? How can you rearrange the composition?

Evaluating

Bloom's original taxonomy was published in 1956. It includes six domain levels, with the pinnacle of learning as 'evaluation'. These domain levels, often visualised in pyramid form, are:

- Evaluation
- Synthesis
- Analysis
- Application
- Comprehension
- Knowledge

Lorin Anderson and David Krathwohl later revised his cognitive taxonomy, placing 'creating' at the top, above 'evaluating'. Their revised taxonomy contains the following levels:

- Creating
- Evaluating
- Analysing
- Applying
- Understanding
- Remembering

These taxonomies are often disputed, as learning is not linear or hierarchical (Berger, 2018). I think both are useful when thinking about evaluating in art if we visualise them together as a circle or cycle because students continually evaluate in art lessons, evaluating information they see as important, why something works or does not, how they can improve, when they need to ask for help or advice and act on it straight away. Some evaluation is a subconscious action, carried out in a split second as decisions are made. Most students will be able to draw on prior knowledge as a metacognitive act, and some will need guidance or reassurance.

Evaluation will not only come at the end of a project in art but at midway points too. Most art teachers will be encouraging students to complete written evaluations, as this is great training for making their learning visible and, for Key Stages 4 and 5, will often form part of evidencing their use of the language of art, craft and design and their ideas. Most art teachers will use 'help sheets' to help teach structures for evaluations, and it should be noted that 'help sheets' should not be used during the ESA (see JCQ, 2024).

Using what went well and why and even better if and why can be helpful. There are many exemplars of different types of 'help sheet' or frameworks to use to teach students evaluation techniques. Students should become familiar with the process, and the idea would be that, after using help sheets a few times, most students could write an evaluation without it.

Plenary tasks

Plenaries may not occur at the end of every lesson but are built into learning cycles. In fact, an art teacher may start the lesson with a plenary. One of my favourite plenaries is the 'walking, talking gallery'. This can be conducted at any appropriate part of the lesson or learning cycle. 'Walking, talking gallery' is where all or selected students' work is laid out, and students walk around to look at the work. They may have a precise question or foci to look at and share verbally or use Post-it notes. Feedback from students can be verbal; looking at artworks as they walk around the classroom will create discussion among the students, even without being given a key question or foci. Just listen. You will hear them calling to each other sharing what they observe and think. I display GCSE students' half-finished final pieces and give Key Stage 3 students Post-it-notes in two colours: one to use to write what they really like and why and another to write a suggestion of what they think could be improved, why or how. They love this task.

I ask students at a midway point to move back from their artwork or hold it up for them to view from a greater distance. In the settings I have worked, this will often result in students frowning or smiling with a nod. No words at first. The smile and nod are the student's (often subconscious) metacognition, evaluating their artwork, evidence of learning, progress or achievement. A frown often means they are questioning how it looks and why – this too is evaluation, isn't it? At any point, I would ask further per-sonalised questions based on the student's ability or journey through the task.

Self/peer marking

I have a distinct memory of being a newly qualified teacher. The Headteacher was my mentor, and I was showing him examples of my marking of Key Stage 3 books. I taught 14 Key Stage 3 classes, as well as GCSE. He asked me if I thought my detailed level of marking (which all students had responded to practically) was sustainable? He told me students are incredibly good at marking each other's and their own work. They will surprisee you with their honesty. I often hear his voice.

I use a variety of self-marking and peer marking. It could be verbal or written. At Key Stage 4, it is worth noting students cannot write in each other's books, but they can use Post-it-notes. White boards could also be used, but this can mean the students who want to use their peer's comments cannot keep them to refer to, hence my preference for Post-it-notes.

Learning diaries

These may have different names: learning journal, learning log, or reflection log (Howe, 2019). Their commonality is they all aim to encourage students to record what they have learnt. There is no right or wrong way to do this in an art lesson, and again, art teachers will know their cohorts. It could be pre-printed with specific questions or just a space where students reflect or answer a question from the board. It is worth noting that they are only useful if the student completes them to their best ability and teachers review or look at them (I do not mean marking).

I do not always have a 'do now' or starter activities for each lesson; these are built into learning cycles. In all key stages, I train students to be able to come in and get on with a task to enable them to experience sustained working. Learning diaries support students to remember what they need to start with. I might write prompts on the board 'Next lesson, I need to remember to...' and give a list of options or they use their own. This is vital in building independent thinking and working.

Conclusion

Declarative knowledge (knowing about things), procedural knowledge (knowing how to do things) and conditional knowledge (knowing the when and why of cognition) can be seen and represented as students produce artwork and making some of the learning visible as metacognition will build habits for students to draw on in future learning and making.

If metacognition is visible, when students are stuck, they know to draw on a previously learnt or experienced strategies. A few years ago, during the ESA period, a colleague asked one of my GCSE students (who had forgotten her sketchbook) what she was doing. This was about five minutes into the lesson, and she was sitting at a desk with a couple of art magazines she had collected on the table and a blank piece of paper. She had previously been developing her own ideas in response to the exam board theme. She replied, 'I don't know'. To my colleague, this meant she did not know what to do. However, five minutes later, she was jotting down ideas by doodling and annotating, tearing out pages of the magazine and creating a collage. At the end of the double lesson, she had produced three ideas for a final piece by using a combination of drawing, collage and written notes. When I asked her what she meant when she told the teacher she did not know what she was doing, she replied 'I did not know what I was doing for my final piece yet, I was thinking'. Her metacognition and learning were not visible or audible for my colleague.

Metacognition happens all the time in art. Eisner said, 'making art takes a lot of thought' (Eisner, 2002), just ask a student 'what made you think of/do that?'. Draw out deeper thinking with because or why. With a confidence in using the language of art and design, students will be able to explain. Often, students' artwork will be the metacognitive outcome or the communication visually demonstrating they selected their ideas, chosen materials, tools and technique, colour scheme and composition to combine and create an outcome. Indeed, creative thinking is a metacognitive process. Explicitly labelling metacognition can support and value the learning journey in art, and weaving metacognition teaching habits into our own practice will support students to know what to do when faced with a new challenge (EEF, 2021).

References

BBC Bitesize. (n.d.). SCAMPER model of creativity, explained|an easy innovation framework for business [GUIDE]. *BiteSize Learning*. Available at: https://www.bitesizelearning.co.uk/resources/scamper-model-creativity (Accessed 1 September 2024).

Berger, R. (2018). Here's what's wrong with bloom's taxonomy: A deeper learning perspective. *Education Week*, section Teaching & Learning. Available at: https://www.edweek.org/teaching-learning/opinion-heres-whats-wrong-with-blooms-taxonomy-a-deeper-learning-perspective/2018/03 (Accessed 7 September 2024).

Carney, P. (2024). The role of metacognition in the art & design GCSE externally set assignment. In N. Burns (Ed.), *Teaching Hacks: Fixing Everyday Classroom Issues With Metacognition*. London: Sage.

Department for Education [DfE]. (2013a). *National Curriculum - Key Stage 3 Art And Design*. Available at: https://assets.publishing.service.gov.uk/media/5a7c4e02ed915d3d0e87b798/SECONDARY_national_curriculum_-_Art_and_design.pdf (Accessed 8 September 2024).

Department for Education [DfE]. (2013b). *National Curriculum in England: Art and Design Programmes of Study*. Available at: https://www.gov.uk/government/publications/national-curriculum-in-england-art-and-design-programmes-of-study/national-curriculum-in-england-art-and-design-programmes-of-study#key-stage-3 (Accessed 1 September 2024).

Education Endowment Foundation. (2021). *Guidance Report Metacognition and Self-Regulated Learning*. Available at: https://d2tic4wvo1iusb.cloudfront.net/production/eef-guidance-reports/metacognition/EEF_Metacognition_and_self-regulated_learning.pdf?v=1731859461 (Accessed 1 September 2024).

Eisner, E. W. (2002). *The Arts and the Creation of Mind.* New Haven, CT: Yale University Press.

Howe, E. E. (2019). Does metacognitive reflection benefit art students? *International Dialogues on Education Journal*, 6(2). https://doi.org/10.53308/ide.v6i2.65

JCQ. (2024). *Instructions for Conducting Non-Examination Assessments (GCE & GCSE Specifications)*, ed. by JCQ. Available at: https://www.jcq.org.uk/wp-content/uploads/2024/08/Instructions_NEA_24-25_FINAL.pdf (Accessed 6 October 2024).

Jia, X., Li, W., & Cao, L. (2019). The role of metacognitive components in creative thinking. *Frontiers in Psychology*, 10, 2404. https://doi.org/10.3389/fpsyg.2019.02404

McNulty, N. (2024). Metacognition in education. *Medium.* Available at: https://medium.com/@niall.mcnulty/metacognition-in-education-c1125b52ed2c (Accessed 1 September 2024).

Ofsted. (2023). *Research Review Series: Art and Design.* Available at: https://www.gov.uk/government/publications/research-review-series-art-and-design/research-review-series-art-and-design (Accessed 1 September 2024).

Pearson. (2016). *GCSE (9-1) Art and Design Component 2 Scheme of Work GCSE Art and Design (2016) Component 2 Scheme of Work.* Available at: https://qualifications.pearson.com/content/dam/pdf/GCSE/Art%20and%20Design/2016/teaching-and-learning-materials/gcse-art-and-design-component-2-sow-updated.pdf (Accessed 14 September 2024).

15

Modern foreign languages

Liam Bretag

Introduction

There are many challenges facing teachers of modern foreign languages (MFL) that those of us who teach the subject know only too well. To be greeted at the classroom door on a Friday afternoon with the repetitive 'Why do we have to learn German?' or 'Why doesn't everyone speak the same language?' is something that we are well versed in replying to with our countless reasons as to why one should learn a foreign language. However, if we were to bypass the general apathy and look for an explanation as to why students feel like this, it is often the case that it is the perceived difficulty of the subject that puts them off. For instance, we are teaching students the grammar and vocabulary of a second language, when they may already be experiencing difficulties in acquiring their own language. Students with low reading ages or issues with literacy may dread this subject because they are already aware that they are going to struggle because they know how much they find their English lessons difficult. Some students without any additional learning needs may already be switched-off to the idea of embracing a new culture due to a preconceived mindset or attitude towards learning a foreign language that makes them opt out. Any additional areas of difficulty will then only support their viewpoint that language learning is unnecessary.

Students who do not possess additional learning needs may find learning a language challenging; those with additional learning needs may find it even more challenging. The use of metacognitive strategies would therefore be beneficial to all students, to allow them to meet the demands of the MFL curriculum. By lessening the amount of information that students have to cope with at any one point, this allows them to deal with one problem at a time and overcome issues with that specific area so that any problem areas do not become seemingly insurmountable. One of the advantages of the new GCSE specification for MFL set out in 2024 is a reduction in the amount of vocabulary and structures required for students to learn for assessments and an adaptation of exam-style questions means that students can become more effectively prepared during lesson time to tackle these tasks and most importantly – do well on them.

The best outcome we can hope for with the reformed GCSE in MFL is that there are higher rates of success and that students can therefore see that having a GCSE qualification in a language is not something that is out of their grasp. Some may argue that having a language as a pre-programmed 'choice' on their options form at the end of Key Stage 3 is already tackling this issue. I would argue that it isn't; making students do a subject that they don't enjoy or don't see the value in, is, in my view, actually making the problem worse. We need to tackle the issue at Key Stage 3 – in lessons with a review of the teaching and learning that is attempting to empower them to be the next generation of linguists. This starts with considering how much information we are asking them to deal with in their learning and if we can improve their performance by just streamlining our teaching through the use of meta-cognitive instruction methods.

The purpose of this chapter is to provide examples of metacognitive strategies that support the effective acquisition of skills and knowledge of the MFL curriculum.

Planning

Let us first consider strategies relating to planning.

Exam question analysis

As we are all aware, in order maximise the amount of effective teaching that takes place in lessons, students must first understand their starting points. All students will have differing levels of understanding of our subject but more importantly, all students will have achieved different levels of success on previous assessments. In order to focus on filling knowledge gaps, we need to empower students to ascertain the problem areas from their prior learning. These can be divided into two groups: knowledge and skills. The knowledge of a language can be summarised as words, phrases and grammatical constructions on the specification that students are taught to use in speaking, listening, reading and writing activities. The skill part is the application of knowledge and the understanding of how to answer the different types of questions in those four key skill areas.

In preparation for an assessment, students should be looking at their previous assessment as a basis. This means looking at their scores and analysing it with a view to making quick successes on their next assessment. As a starting point for their revision, I would guide students towards the data I have collected, so that they can see their strengths and weaknesses. Student data can be presented in a table on a Question Level Analysis spreadsheet (Table 15.1), where marks are collected per question. Also noted down is the question topic and question style. A simplified version is here as an example.

Table 15.1 A question level analysis spreadsheet

Name	1. Free time	2. Relationships	3. School	4. Environment
	Multiple choice question/4	True/false/not in text/4	Who says what/3	Answers in English/2
Student X	4	2	3	2
Student Y	4	1	1	2
Student Z	3	2	1	2

From the above table, we can see that students achieved full marks on Question 4. This tells me as the teacher that these students' knowledge of the environment topic and their skill in answering questions with the 'Answers in English' style questions is excellent. Students can therefore capitalise on this by revising the methods they used to successfully answer this question. We can also see how students performed less well on Question 2. This suggests that students do not know the relationships topic well and/or they are not fully confident in applying their knowledge to the 'True/False/Not in Text' style questions. With this information, students could then be provided with tasks with the aim of filling in their knowledge gaps of the relationships topic and filling in their skills gaps of True/False/Not in Text questions. They would likely benefit from using mini whiteboards to test vocabulary on the relationships topic – starting with single words and gradually building to full sentences in a variety of tenses and as the teacher, I would base my sentences on all the work they can find in their exercise books. After having their knowledge of vocabulary and structures tested, it would then be helpful for students to test their skills using the same style question on a variety of topics – as the expert, I would first of all be walking students through my thought process and showing them where and how I find the answers. On the second one, students will take a greater role in the modelling of this task – this allows them to gradually become more self-sufficient in answering this type of question. Students would hear me asking questions like 'What am I thinking at this stage?' and 'Would it be fair to say that we should be looking for…?' Then on the third attempt at this style question, students would complete the task independently and in silence and this would ensure they are consolidating this reteaching.

Also useful at this stage is providing students with high quality answers for different question topics and types. Students then work in groups to analyse them and explain to each other what makes them good answers, for example, accurately incorporating a subjunctive clause to discuss where they would like to go on holiday if they had more money.

Strategy evaluation

After the initial stage of first teaching students about a strategy to successfully answer a question, it is helpful to revisit this strategy in the coming weeks and months of the year to see how successfully this strategic approach has been assimilated. In the run up to an assessment, quite often I will have a writing lesson, whereby I will ask students to complete similar tasks to those on the assessment paper. I have always found it advantageous in improving their confidence and resilience to get the students themselves discussing strategy. I will divide the class into groups and give them a writing question – at Key Stage 4 for example, this could be a translation into the target language (important to use homogenous foundation and higher groups if this is the case, as the tasks will be structured slightly differently). I will set them a specific time frame and their task is not to complete the translation, but rather to bullet point their strategy by working together to discuss how they are aiming to be successful when they do complete it. At the end of the task, students will lead the discussion about how they would approach the task and I will facilitate them asking each other questions. We will agree the best strategy and then students will complete the translation independently. Students will peer-mark their work and then we will discuss how successful this strategy has been and whether we could – based on the feedback from the peer-marking – adapt our strategy at all for next time. This can be completed with a variety of tasks and not just at Key Stage 4.

Knowledge organisers

A lot of the time in MFL, it is confidence that holds students back – particularly speaking, but also in writing – the two productive key skill areas. If students do not have a repertoire of vocabulary and structures that are familiar to them that they can recall, they become more flustered and the task becomes much more daunting. This in turn means they are likely to give up. With sentence builders, if used properly, students are empowered to provide accurate, high-level sentences, fulfilling necessary criteria, such as using the correct tense for a bullet point in a role play or 90-word task.

Many teachers may prefer not to use knowledge organisers as they are onerous to create and not used often enough to be worthwhile. I believe repetition is the key to success here. For every single lesson at Key Stage 3, I spend the first 5–10 minutes after the starter task having the sentence builder for the current topic displayed on the board (as well as stuck in exercise books) and I will read a sentence in the target language and students will find the English (written directly underneath) and copy it out onto mini whiteboards. I will count them down in the target language and then they will all show their boards together. After four or five sentences in the target language, I will do another four or five in English and they then need to write in the target language. This is low-stakes, high-gain preparation for learning or retrieval practice (works both before and after a topic is introduced) and students feel more confident. Over the course of the half term (or unit of work), I will start to remove the sentence builder earlier and earlier and in the final few lessons of the topic, students should be doing it without the sentence builder altogether. In the assessment lesson for this topic, I would expect to see greater resilience when it comes to writing in the target language as students have built on that repertoire and feel more confident to be able to produce high-level, accurate sentences to satisfy the grade descriptions.

Monitoring

The following strategies are concerned with monitoring.

Checklists

The use of checklists within MFL lessons can be transformational for students who are either low in confidence or for students who lose focus easily. It gives them something clear to work with that can organise their ideas and ensure they don't miss any key detail. For high levels of success with checklists, it is important to base them on the mark scheme criteria – for example: how are students going to achieve a Grade 9 on the 150-word task on the higher writing paper? Constructing checklists should allow students to easily cross-reference their work with the mark scheme grade descriptors. For example:

- Have I checked for accuracy?
- Have I included all tenses?
- Have I used time phrases and sequencers to complement the various tenses?

Acronyms are also useful to serve the same purpose – a common one for the speaking exam and the foundation writing exam is PALMW for the photo card task – People, Action, Location, Mood, and Weather:

People: *Auf dem Foto gibt es vier Personen.*
Action: *Sie spielen Fußball.*
Location: *Sie sind in einem Park.*
Mood: *Sie sind glücklich.*
Weather: *Es ist sehr sonnig.*

As with many things, the way checklists are successful is with repetition: they should be on the inside cover of exercise books, written in margins, displayed on the MFL corridor and discussed regularly. A retrieval practice starter for key skills lessons could be to ask students to write out the acronym in full and/or provide examples to consolidate their understanding.

Warning signs

For students to achieve greater levels of success independently, teachers need to encourage students to become more self-regulating. This means being able to identify misconceptions at stages before they finish a task so that there are not marks removed for either poor exam skills (not understanding how to answer the question) or lack of knowledge (absence of appropriate vocabulary and/or structures pertaining to the needs of the task). For example, not recognising that the first bullet point requires a response in the past tense or not using topic vocabulary like *Schulregeln*, *Klassenfahrt* or *Mathestunde* in a school topic-based question, will lower marks but could potentially be avoided by using more metacognitive strategies like identifying those warning signs of mistakes and challenging them. This will lead to more self-reflective learning and greater outcomes.

Teachers also have a role in teaching students the explicit ways they can be self-regulating, for instance by live marking in class and immediately spotting errors in a written response and re-writing the sentence to more effectively gain marks. It seems that many schools are now in favour of more of the marking that teachers do to be live and in-lesson, as opposed to marking a set of books once per half term after the work has taken place, when students will have already forgotten about the mistake they made are less likely to learn from it two, three, four (or more) weeks later.

Flow maps

For students who have dyslexia or a low reading age, considering writing an extended piece of writing can be extremely daunting – even with concessions such as extra time. The checklist strategy above, while helpful for some, may prove just as challenging to others as the actual task itself. If checklist information can be converted into a visual flow map for students with literacy difficulties, this could be the first step to success. They may be able to process this information more effectively and therefore retain it for future success in exams. For example, changing PALMW from a big, bold, colourful font on a presentation slide to an actual picture of an open palm displaying the letters P, A, L, M and W may help students to visualise this memory hook and then consequently be able to use it during the exam. In order for students to become well versed with acronyms like this or other checklists, it is useful to have it stuck in exercise books and also displayed in the classroom. It is also sometimes helpful with regards to presenting information to use colour-coded text boxes which provide shortcuts for students who struggle with vast amounts of text, for example – all chunks of information to read in light blue, questions to answer in green and answers in red. This will prompt students to be more alert and recognise the current task.

Evaluating

Let us consider some metacognitive strategies relating to assessment.

Wrappers

I have always made it clear to students that success is not merely determined by carrying out the task itself, rather everything you do beforehand and afterwards. I always use the phrase: Prepare – Write – Check. If we look at the listening assessment in MFL, for example, we know that students will be given allocated time at the beginning of the assessment to read through the question paper and prepare themselves for what they are going to hear via the audio recording. This is crucial for them to pre-empt any answers by narrowing down their choice of potential options – this is the PREPARE stage. For example, a question may require a student to listen to a discussion about holiday preferences and the task is to allocate a holiday type to a person. Where the holiday types are listed in a table, at this point students would be annotating the paper. By doing this, they know that if they hear *Strandurlaub*, they will allocate 'beach holiday' to this person or question number. It is important to remind students that there are numerous other ways in this might be the right answer. Students need to remember that 'by the sea' or 'on the coast' could also refer to this answer. Once they have had the preparation period, they will need to answer the question. They will do this using their knowledge and skills acquired in lessons to make the right choice in answering. This is the WRITE stage. Afterwards, during the CHECK stage, they will need to ensure all questions have been answered and that they make sense.

The purpose of the Prepare – Write – Check process is that it makes it clear to students that they can perform better on tasks when they think more strategically. Also, when it comes to evaluating our success, students are able to make clear points as to where they could have improved at each stage. This will usually take the form of a simple table on an A5 piece of paper which contains questions like the following for each section:

Prepare:

'How long did you spend reading the questions at the beginning?'

'Did you recognise that you need to answer in German for this section?'

Write:

'Did you notice that in Question 10, the man talks about his friend's hobbies, before his own?'

'Did you remember that *fast* is a false friend in German?'

Check:

'Did you check that you had answered all questions before the end of the assessment?'

'Did you ensure there was enough detail in your worded answers?'

Self-/peer-marking

The most effective feedback that I have seen has always included a blend of self-, peer- and teacher-led marking. The reason for this is simple – students need teachers to provide quality written feedback for extended responses and assessments, but they do not need their input for vocab tests, short listening tasks or multiple-choice questions in class. It would suffice for students to self-mark these types of activities, as it is a case of simply writing a tick or a cross and a score in the margin. Students are then able to write a brief summary as to why they think they went wrong and a target to improve on their next task. Peer-marking is for shorter speaking and writing tasks where a different perspective is required. These two key skill areas offer flexibility and so are more open to interpretation, as opposed to the listening and reading key skill areas which is much more objectively right or wrong. I always emphasise the importance of good quality feedback in peer-marking as this helps the students to be more aware of their own strengths and weaknesses. The benefit is not only for the student whose book is being marked, but also for the student who is marking. Similar to how mentoring an ITT student is not only helpful for the ITT student, but also for the mentor as it makes them question their own practice and brings alternative ways of teaching into their own practice.

Some of the best examples of self-marking takes place during a feedback lesson after an assessment. When students are issued with a whole-class feedback sheet, they are able to first of all see the strengths and areas to improve but crucially have the opportunity to make targets for the next unit of work based on their performance on the assessment that they have just sat. Non-examples of effective targets are:

- Revise more
- Write 90 words [i.e. target amount, as opposed to fewer]
- Check my work

Instead, these target should be more like:

- Revise vocabulary on the town topic to ensure I have a variety of language to use.
- Improve the quantity of my writing by including more opinions and/or reasons.
- Thoroughly check my work so that I avoid careless errors, like using an infinitive verb instead of a past participle.

Where there is self- or peer-marking, teachers should quality assure the process. It is important to ensure it is being done meaningfully otherwise it becomes a waste of time. When done properly, self- and peer-marking supports metacognition as it breaks down concepts to clearly provide guidance for success on the subsequent topics and assessments. Students can refer back to this and use it as a success criteria, along with the notion of 'plan – write – check'.

Good, better, best answers

In order for students to understand how to form their answers, especially at the start of their Key Stage 4 journey, it is imperative that they see exemplars for the task, or a WAGOLL – What A Good One Looks Like. They are usually best formed by a teacher because they can be customised so that they contain all the good parts you would like to exemplify. This is especially the case for speaking and writing tasks where marks rely heavily on students' constructions of answers. An effective way of introducing the speaking and writing assessment tasks is to provide students with exemplars that contain very subtle differences. In groups and having been provided with the mark schemes, students would then work together to decide which answer is 'good', 'better', and 'best'. By having this as a student-led task, they are themselves discovering what the mark scheme looks like and how very subtle differences can sometimes mean the difference of a whole grade. Once students have done this task, it is then advantageous to ask them to mark it. I would usually provide different coloured highlighters for them to examine the parts that accrue marks as per the different parts of the assessment criteria for that task, for example with a 150-word task, highlighting all the examples of different tenses in one colour. If you have a higher ability group, a further task would be to ask them to circle all the mistakes and make suggestions for what to add. After this task is complete, I ask students to use the best example as a writing frame – along with their suggestions – to write their own version. This is then 'version 0' and they have a basis of what this task should look like moving forwards for each different topic.

It is sometimes helpful to turn this on its head: provide students with a WABOLL – What A Bad One Looks Like, including all the errors that class has made and it can turn into a feedback and re-teaching lesson where students are able to identify the very mistakes they have been making and to then understand why it is wrong. A typical example of what to include is using *haben* instead of *sein* as the auxiliary verb in the perfect tense with movement, e.g., *Letztes Jahr habe ich nach Frankreich gefahren.* Unlike the WAGOLL task, I would only provide one WABOLL example, instead of three, and I would ask them to mark it, circling and correcting mistakes such as this.

Conclusion

The teaching of MFL is growing in importance. In an ever-changing world, being able to communicate with other people in a different language provides so many benefits – as we are all fully aware, not least giving our students the ability to boost their confidence, develop their problem-solving skills and increase their knowledge of their first language. Despite how much we are passionate about teaching our subject and the sense of success we get when students are finally able to conjugate a verb fully, this doesn't remove the challenges we face. The strategies listed in this chapter seek to provide supportive methods for teachers of MFL to break down barriers for students to enable the successful assimilation of knowledge and skills across the MFL curriculum, through less cognitively challenging and more meaningful tasks that promote success for all key stages, year groups and ability levels.

16

The tutor curriculum and metacognition

Nathan Burns

Introduction

How metacognition fits in with tutor time may not be something that you would be expecting in a curriculum facing book. However, as schools continue to focus on marginal gains for progress, eyes often turn to tutor time. With students typically having a tutor period every day of the week, the cumulative time spent in this environment is significant – often more than most other subjects that students are studying, even during Key Stage 4 while studying GCSEs. Due to this, tutor periods are no longer typically exempt from a curriculum. I've never worked in, or with, a school that allows tutor time to be 'dead'. Instead, activities are pencilled in for each day of the week, from assemblies, through to silent reading, homework to behaviour conversations, and everything in between. Due to the advancement of a tutor curriculum, it means that the same considerations, around coherency, consistency, big aims and skill development, requirements for all high-quality curricula, need to be considered. In the same breath, it means that a tutor curriculum provides a high-quality opportunity to develop metacognitive skills of students, thus supporting their metacognitive development in other curriculum areas, as well as their general attainment outcomes. In summary, tutor periods provide a yet 'untapped' opportunity within the school timetable to establish the teaching and development of metacognitive abilities for students.

However, the one main difference with the tutor curriculum is the lack of consistency between schools. Where two English departments, separated by hundreds of miles, will be similar in their curriculum topic areas, due to guidance by the National Curriculum, no such thing exists, at this point, for the tutor curriculum. Therefore, this chapter will attempt to provide a plethora of occasions where these metacognitive strategies can be utilised effectively within a tutor curriculum, aiming to include at least one example that corresponds with what your tutor curriculum currently includes.

Planning

Let's look at metacognitive strategies that support planning.

Flow maps

The first strategy is one that can be used on so many different occasions. Often, a flow map is used to support SEN students in their sequencing of work. However, as we know, high quality teaching for SEN students, is actually just high-quality teaching for all students.

One way in which this strategy can be used in tutor time is to help students to determine the order in which they need to complete their work. Students could try to use a diary (if your school still uses one), or potentially make a list of everything that they have to do. However, a simpler way, as well as a more visually helpful way of doing this, is to produce a flow map. This map would include all tasks that need to be done, and place them in the order that they need to be completed. It could focus just on schools' tasks that need to be completed, such as homework, or could incorporate wider tasks which need to be done, such as any chores at home. The benefit here is dual. Firstly, students are forced to prioritise tasks that they need to complete, hopefully reducing the likelihood of choosing a lower priority task just because it is 'easier' or more 'fun' to complete, and instead focussing on the highest priority task. The second main benefit is the visual aspect, which I find, from experience, is easier for students to follow than a homework diary. A third, additional benefit, is that it helps students to balance home life and school work, as well.

This strategy can also be encouraged in students when they are completing homework during tutor time, as many students do. Students can use the flow map as a planning grid, to write out the order in which they are going to complete stages of a task – for example, the stages of a mathematical problem or the steps through which they will work to decode a poem. Here, the use of the strategy slows students down, placing emphasis on the importance of planning, and getting students to think clearly about the order in which they need to complete a task to give themselves the best opportunity of success.

Key word quizzing

Regardless of the subject area that you teach, you will find one common issue in your students' responses to questions, which is poor comprehension of questions. As a mathematics teacher by trade, I'm all too familiar with the reading level required to access the GCSE papers, and equally as aware of the many, many dozens of subject terminologies (whether those be questioning words, or subject specific words) that students are supposed to be aware of. This phenomenon is not unique to maths, either – it's across the board. Reading levels expectations are high, the questioning words used plentiful, and the abundance of subject specific terminology significant, regardless of the subject that you teach. Key word quizzing therefore provides an opportunity for students to develop their vocabulary, becoming more comfortable with the range of terminology that is used and that they are expected to know. Additionally, improving key word knowledge will improve comprehension (as not knowing key words is majorly problematic to comprehension, of course), which in turn provides significant opportunity for increased student attainment.

There are a few ways to go about this during a tutor time. Firstly, it may be students already have a bank of key words that they have been provided with, or have developed during their different subject lessons. If this is the case, students can self-test on these key words, by covering up the definition and then writing down or verbalising what they believe it is, before checking, or, students can peer test, questioning one another on these key word definitions. On other occasions, students may not have a bank of key words that they need to know. In this circumstance, it may be that students do have knowledge organisers for their different subjects, and can use these to develop their own bank of key words. Once done, students can self or peer test in the same way as mentioned above.

If students do not have a list, and cannot glean a list from any documents they have, such as a knowledge organiser, then there are a couple of further options. The first is that, upon seeing this strategy, a senior leader requests that all subject leads develop a bank of key words that students need to know, and that these are provided to students, as mentioned in the first strategy above. There is a workload associated to this, but often exam boards provide lists of exam key words, while subject key words are often determined in a subjects scheme of work. If these are available, the workload should be significantly reduced. However, if you did not want to go down this route, students could instead be provided with, or encouraged to get, a small notebook where they record down key words from their subjects. These could be key words that all students must know, or words that an individual student has failed to comprehend, and so needs to work on them in order to keep pace with the learning of a lesson. This strategy is nice as it places ownership of key word development onto students, as well as removing a task from teachers.

If you did go for this final option, you may get students to research definitions for their key words from dictionaries, during tutor time, if they do not already have them, or if they do (or once done!), students can again self-test or peer test, as outlined above.

Knowledge organisers

This strategy may be one that you very quickly skim through if you are not a school that uses knowledge organisers (or drivers, or whatever name you may otherwise assign to them!), but if you are, then this section is crucial!

In my experience with knowledge organisers, both as a teacher, consultant, training and researcher, knowledge organisers are all too often time-sucking creations that end up being static. The time taken to create them was not worth it, as they become stuck in students' books, never to see the light of day again. The theory behind knowledge organisers is strong, which is why so many schools brought them in, but, in the rush to create these documents, exactly how they could be used, and why they needed to look different across subject areas, was forgotten. There is hope, however, in the form of tutor time!

As mentioned in the previous strategy, poor comprehension, driven by a lack of knowledge or understanding of key words, is a barrier to student outcomes. The other barrier (which is obvious), is an individual's declarative knowledge. If students do not know the correct facts, figures, quotes, and so forth, then they will, once again, struggle to access and complete tasks successfully. As established in the very first chapter of this book, one significant area of an individual's knowledge of cognition is their knowledge of self – that is the required knowledge to complete a task successfully.

Knowledge organisers were designed to support with this area, and if used successfully, can be. One of the very best ways to use them during tutor time is for students to self-test – covering over key dates, quotes or other pieces of knowledge – and then seeing what they can recall. This low stakes way of quizzing is extremely powerful. Though it may not seem very metacognitive, it is actually extremely metacognitive. Students need to identify their own knowledge of self – what information is it from the knowledge organiser that they do not know, but need to know? Once this has been determined, students can self-test and fill in these self-determined gaps in their understanding.

A further option is for students to make flashcards, but this is often a 'good' way to actually avoid getting to the self-testing (a hand covering information or a sheet partially folded is often sufficient). Equally, students can peer test, asking each other questions, which can be helpful at speeding up the process, but can lead to greater volume levels in the classroom and lower participation levels. How you go about using this with your tutor group, is up to you!

Monitoring

Here are some metacognitive strategies related to monitoring.

Checklists

So often, metacognitive strategies look different in different curriculum areas. Metacognition of course hinges upon cognition, so where this changes, so does the metacognitive strategy and what it looks like. One area where this is less true, however, is when an individual is monitoring their thinking, meaning that the strategies proposed here should work really well for all students, and for all of the subjects which they are studying.

The first of those strategies is a really simple one – checklists. When completing tasks, due to the cognitive loads placed on us – effective recall of procedural and declarative knowledge to start with – it is very easy to forget to include certain things within a response. Our mind is focussing on decoding other information, successfully using a strategy and staying within a time limit. Students can be trained, during a tutor time, that when they are completing tasks, they should first produce a checklist of everything that they need to include, or do, in order to be successful with their task completion.

This is a strategy that will likely be taught within subject time, but is a very straight-forward one for a tutor to teach, or remind students, of. Whenever students are completing homework during their tutor time, their tutor should remind them, and encourage them, to note down a little checklist of all of the things that they need to do. Once they have been done, they can then be ticked off to ensure that the student is staying on track with their task.

The important thing with this strategy, as with all other metacognitive strategies, is that it is rooted within content. Therefore, tutors should look to explain this within the content of a homework task, rather than as a standalone theory.

This strategy is also an effective one as a planning strategy, so there is no reason why tutors couldn't encourage it for students when they are planning their approach to tasks, or if they are making a to do list. As the strategy works so effectively across all subject areas, it is a good one to encourage in the tutor room!

Key questions

This strategy requires a little more subject knowledge, but is a superb skill to help to develop independent learners. So often, students are faced with longer tasks and:

- Give up before they have even got started.
- Do some of the task and then just stop.
- Get cognitively lost in the requirement of a task and do not complete all of it.

Developing an individual's ability to break down a longer task into shorter, more manageable chunks, as this strategy proposes, is a wonderful way to negate this. Once again, it is likely to be used in tutor time when students are completing homework. As it is a more subject specific strategy (how a question is broken down in maths is different to a coursework task in art, for example) means that as a tutor, you should focus on encouraging students to break down tasks, rather than doing it for them. The process of breaking down a larger task into smaller manageable chunks is a huge step forward for a lot of students, and will really develop their independence.

The main benefit of this strategy is that if it becomes a commonly used strategy in tutor time, and one that is spoken about a lot, it becomes second nature to students, and hence something that significantly supports their independent learning. When students are at home completing their work, they have a strategy to turn to in order to break down longer tasks, when they no longer have an expert there to help them!

The other benefit of this type of strategy is it supports comprehension. By getting students to break down a question or task into its components, they are really being forced to think about what exactly the task is asking them to do. For example, a student may be asked to *'explain what Christians believe in'*, which is a very deep (and potentially long) question. However, this could be broken down into: Holy book, place of worship, religion formation story, key dates, and key individuals. The ability to break down this task into smaller sub-questions will likely develop an individual's comprehension abilities.

Warning signs

Whenever I do training around developing metacognitive monitoring in students, I always come back to this strategy. It doubles up as the most superb metacognitive monitoring strategy, but also as a brilliant way to develop awareness of misconceptions, strengthening a student's subject understanding significantly.

This is one strategy which certainly is subject dependent – even topic and question dependent. Every time the cognition changes, so will the misconceptions. Exactly what these misconceptions are is of course the domain of the subject teacher. However, that does not make this strategy redundant within a tutor curriculum. Rather, a tutor can actively be encouraging students to think about misconceptions that they know can crop up within a topic – for example, not having common denominators when adding or subtracting fractions.

Of course, the tutor is unlikely to have the subject expertise, so how exactly do they go about supporting their tutees? There are a number of questions that they can ask.

- Are there any misconceptions that your teacher mentioned during the lesson?
- Are there any misconceptions mentioned on the knowledge organiser or in your book?
- Did you make any mistakes during the lesson that you now know you need to avoid?
- What are some of the mistakes that your teacher modelled?
- Can you give some examples of answers that would be *obviously* wrong (e.g., a negative answer for the length of a rectangle)?

There may be other questions that you can think of too, and as you start to do this during a tutor time, you'll develop a repertoire of questions which work for you! However you go about it, the benefits can be large. By encouraging students to think about the common mistakes that are made and misconceptions that are shown, they are actively aware of what should *not* be in their answer. Equally, from a monitoring point of view, if any of these issues crop up in their responses, they will know that they need to make changes now, rather than ploughing on until the end of the task, where they will be evaluating their work.

Evaluation

Let us now turn to look at strategies of evaluation.

Answering directed questions

We all know how important evaluation is. If we do not evaluate, we won't be able to identify areas for improvement, nor will we be able to identify our strengths (which is just as important, if not more so). Poor, or non-existent evaluation means that students learning will be ineffective and inefficient – the strides forward that they could be making, just won't be happening. The issues however, with evaluation, is it is easy to 'complete' at a very surface level. 'Next time I will revise more'; 'next time I will actually try', 'I knew it I just didn't read the question properly'. These are all phrases that we will have heard student(s) use at some point in time. Getting students to engage at a deeper, and more meaningful level, is difficult (to say the least)!

One way which this can be done successfully during tutor time is through the use of directed questions. There are copious opportunities for students to use this technique, including:

- When looking over summative assessments
- When reviewing homeworking feedback
- When reviewing lessons from the day or the week
- When consider other feedback that has been provided
- When reviewing revision progress

Tutor time provides a great opportunity for students to take some time to answer some directed questions around the areas flagged above. Often curriculum time is so short that there isn't the potential to do it within lesson time, but it remains crucial to provide students the opportunity to reflect at a deeper level.

Having established the opportunities for students to answer directed questions during a tutor time, you will also need some questions to direct to students!

- One
- Two

There are a few things to consider with this strategy. It may be that questions can be pre-printed and then given out to students whenever you see them doing some evaluation of their own work. Equally, it might be something that is timetabled in on a certain day each week, and students are required to bring along a piece of work to reflect on. It may even be that this is timetabled into the tutor curriculum after whole year assessments, so that students are all able to do the same directed questions for the same piece of work, at the same time. It's often easier if all students are answering questions at the same time!

New Strategy

This strategy is certainly one of the more unpopular ones with students, because it involves them having to just repeat the work that they have just done – but with very good reason. Upon repeating the work, students of course have to use an alternative strategy, forcing them to consider alternative approaches, and allowing them to consider the relative strengths, weaknesses and efficiencies of different strategies. As students become more comfortable with alternative strategies, they become more flexible learners, thus improving their problem-solving abilities. However, without a solid push, students are not going to, off their own back, repeat work with an alternative strategy.

The benefits of this strategy are huge, and though it can often be prioritised during subject teaching time, there is not always the time to do it. Thus, tutor time becomes a very good opportunity! There are some considerations there, mainly around how students will be able to recall the alternative strategy is they are not in lesson with their subject teacher.

A few things can be done. Firstly, if procedures and models are provided on a knowledge organiser, then students will be able to use this to support them in answering the question with an alternative strategy. If that is not available, then students could instead make sure that they have copied down an example, from the lesson, of how the alternative strategy is used. Then, they will be able to use this model to guide them. Again, where this is not a possibility, students can engage with online resources, as recommended by their class teacher, or they may instead look to get a peer to teach them, or check over how they have used that alternative strategy.

Positively, when students are using this technique, they already know what the answer should look like or be, having already completed it once. Therefore, the next time around should not be content difficult, as all students are having to focus on is the strategy that they are using!

A particularly good time to use this strategy is in the run up to assessments. Students can revise topics by using this strategy, ensuring that they have as many tools at their disposal, and are as flexible and prepared for the assessments as they can be. Another good time to encourage students to do this is straight after they have completed work where there are two obvious strategies available to them – for example, solving equations with brackets in Maths. It may even be possible for Heads of Year to coordinate with Heads of Department to identify suitable topics, where students will have all of the information and modelling that they need, so tutors know exactly when to be encouraging students to be using this technique!

Learning diaries

The final strategy that can be used in a tutor curriculum is possibly the most straight forward – the learning diary. The best way for this diary to be used is if it is completed on a set day each week, or a set time each day, and all students are doing it at the same time. The more frequently it can be done, the better too, so that students are recording down key evaluation points closer to the time of making them. For example, recalling information several days after deducing it is going to be very difficult, and will likely lack the specificity required.

Learning diaries should follow a common format, typically focussing in on one area of strength and one area of development, that a student has deduced. This could be done in a small exercise book, notepad, or a pre-printed booklet for students. This need not take long, either, as this is a short period of evaluation.

Crucially, this strategy will need to be modelled to students, and followed-up, within the tutor period, will be needed. Without any of these things, it will once again be very easy for students to be superficial with their evaluation, leaving the diary as a pointless activity. Therefore, to begin, the tutor will need to model what accurate recording of a strength and area for improvement looks like, as well as the type of language that students should be using, and the depth to the conclusions. For example, 'I didn't get fractions', will become 'I struggled with adding together fractions because I keep forgetting to simplify them at the end'. This instantly becomes more thoughtful, and helpful, evaluation, that will be useful for future progress. Tutors should provide sentence starters, and guidance too, where appropriate and necessary. Beyond this, tutors will need to walk their rooms, ensuring that students are going in to depth and not being superficial in their evaluations. To begin with, this may feel like a significant amount of work, and there may be resistance from students – but it is all about habit forming. Once the learning diary is a consistently used part of the tutor curriculum, it will become second nature, and the need to 'check-up' on students will reduce.

Beyond this, there will also be a need to use this evaluation – otherwise even the very best conclusions will become static and cede the task a waste of time! These diaries could, as an example, be used to support the planning strategies mentioned at the very start of this chapter, for example. Equally, in the run up to exams, students would be able to go through their diaries and identify key areas that the need to work on prior to their assessment – improving their knowledge of self.

Conclusion

Tutor time is growing in importance and provides a wonderful opportunity to further develop students within our schools. Within this, a tutor curriculum, becoming more and more common-place across schools, provides a wonderous opportunity to develop the metacognitive skills of our students. Though tutor time cuts across the range of academic subjects, there are still strategies, like those implemented in this chapter, that can be effectively introduced and incorporated into the tutor curriculum, to support the development of student metacognitive skills. Implementation will need to be context specific, considering the time available, the resources at hand and the aims of the whole school, but there is merit in introducing these strategies into your tutor time curriculum.

Index